MUSCLE LOGIC

MUSCLE LOGIC

ESCALATING DENSITY TRAINING

CHANGES THE RULES FOR MAXIMUM-IMPACT WEIGHT TRAINING

CHARLES STALEY

RODALE

Rodale books may be purchased for business or promotional use or for special sales.
For information, please write to:
Special Markets Department, Rodale Inc., 733 Third Avenue, New York, NY 10017

Printed in the United States of America
Rodale Inc. makes every effort to use acid-free ♾, recycled paper ♻.

Photographs by Mitch Mandel / Rodale Images
Book design by Susan P. Eugster

Library of Congress Cataloging-in-Publication Data

Staley, Charles.
Muscle logic : escalating density training changes the rules for maximum-impact weight training / Charles Staley.
p. cm.
Includes index.
ISBN-13 978–1–60529–634–0 hardcover
ISBN-10 1–60529–634–1 hardcover
ISBN-13 978–1–59486–083–6 paperback
ISBN-10 1–59486–083–1 paperback
1. Bodybuilding. 2. Weight training. 3. Muscle strength. I. Title.
GV546.5.S73 2005
613.7'13—dc22 2005021208

Distributed to the trade by Macmillan

2 4 6 8 10 9 7 5 3 1 hardcover
4 6 8 10 9 7 5 paperback

RODALE
LIVE YOUR WHOLE LIFE™

We inspire and enable people to improve their lives and the world around them

For more of our products visit **rodalestore.com** or call 800-848-4735

ACKNOWLEDGMENTS

THE PROCESS OF WRITING A BOOK SUCH AS THIS ONE IS MUCH LIKE a massive iceberg, which is largely submerged and unseen: The visible portion is in your hands; now I'd like to reveal and acknowledge the less-visible-yet-crucial people behind the scenes who truly made this book possible.

To Rebecca: Your limitless love and support mean more to me than words can express. Thank you for providing the stability in my life that allows me to pursue my life's work.

To Ashleigh: My one wish for you is to know that personal achievement, especially when it enriches the lives of others, is the true source of happiness. Despite all the great things that have happened to me in my life, being your dad is the greatest!

To Julianne: You have been the glue that's held my business together for the past 2 years—thank you for your dedication and hard work.

To Zach Schisgal and Courtney Conroy at Rodale: I owe you both a debt of gratitude for your help, support, and direction with this project. Thanks for helping me get this important message out to so many people.

To Tim Patterson: I want the world to know that EDT wouldn't have come this far without a pivotal phone conversation we had a few years back—thanks for all you've taught me.

Finally, I want to express my sincere gratitude to Dr. Sal Arria and Dr. Fred Hatfield, who provided me with my start in this industry. No one would have ever heard of Charles Staley without these two men.

INTRODUCTION

WHENEVER I'M BROWSING THROUGH A BOOK AT THE BOOKSTORE, I tend to quickly scan through the introduction, not really expecting to find anything "meaty" until the main part of the book.

So let me get right down to brass tacks and throw you something meaty, right here, right now—weight training works, but it can work a whole lot better than the way you're *used* to doing it!

I make no apologies for my bluntness in making this statement. Most gym rats are almost comically inefficient in the weight room—this includes professional and Olympic athletes, by the way. The inefficiency stems from the common belief, be it conscious or unconscious, that pain is the main goal of a workout. In fact, almost every serious weight trainer I've ever met actually gauges the value of each workout based on how sore it made him the next day. Sound familiar?

If you did anything else in life this way, you'd fail in a spectacular way. Could you imagine a chiropractor or an accountant or a bank teller organizing her day so that she was as tired as possible at quitting time? If people actually did this, you'd hear conversations like this at the water cooler:

"Wow, yesterday really kicked my tail. I could hardly move this morning!"

"Yeah, you're not kidding—by the time I got home, I felt like I'd been hit by a truck!"

Okay, this comparison is admittedly a bit silly, but the point remains valid nonetheless:

Your *performance* in the gym, *not* the pain, soreness, or fatigue that can result from that performance, is what determines the quality of your results.

If you're completely new to weight training, most of what you'll read in the pages that follow will simply strike you as commonsense logic.

On the other hand, if you're a veteran gym rat, I think—actually, I *know*—much of what you're about to learn will be a radical departure from pretty much every weight-training system you've ever tried or read about.

Although I've provided a number of sample training programs later in the book, there's room for plenty of creativity. In fact, once you've read the book and experienced the workouts, I strongly urge you to "color outside the lines" as you find new, creative ways to apply EDT to your workouts.

EDT has changed the lives—and minds!—of many thousands of people who have experienced mind-blowing progress in record time, even after months (or in some cases years) of stagnation.

Read the following pages with an open mind, and get ready to grow like never before.

Oh—one last thing: When people ask you what you're "on," tell them you're on EDT!

WHAT PEOPLE ARE SAYING ABOUT EDT

"The sheer effectiveness and brutality of the EDT program does not come across in the written word. This is a total *gym experience."*

—ALWYN COSGROVE, CSCS
Director of Cosgrove Results Fitness, Newhall, California

"I have always bounced around going from 'the next best thing for fat loss' and other 3-month-long training programs. I always burned out. The workouts got boring. Before I found EDT, I weighed about 270 to 275 pounds. I thought that light weights were for toning and heavy weights were for bulking. Which one should I do? In reading about EDT, I found that the answer was simple.

"After experiencing EDT, I could talk in hyperbole and keywords. Paradigm shift. The principle of progressive overload. Prioritization. These are all great describers of EDT principles, but these cool-sounding phrases do not capture the core of Escalating Density Training.

"When I look at what I have to do in a given day, my training is the one time of the day when I do not *want to think. EDT, in a sense, embraces this,* my *ideal workout.*

"This intuitive packaging allows me to focus. Concentrate on nothing.

"This intensity makes a lot of sense, but it is the first training methodology I have stuck with for an extended period of time.

"As a result, I have dropped nearly 50 pounds of fat, put on approximately 5 pounds of muscle, and increased my strength and conditioning levels dramatically in less than 6 months. Moreover, my body fat percentage plummeted to 16 to 17 percent from 29 percent.

"My best friends now ask me for training advice. A buddy's girlfriend has dropped her spinning classes for a fat-loss EDT program. They tell me to get new clothes, but I am afraid to, because I will have to buy more after another 6 months.

"When someone at the gym asks you how many sets you have left, you will respond in minutes or seconds. Never mind the quizzical looks—you are experiencing results.

"I experienced the same, along with an increased sense of self-awareness and confidence.

"My morning EDT workouts get me going for the rest of my day, as the training philosophies learned with EDT will influence my training for my lifetime."

—TONY POST

"One thing that attracted me to EDT was that I would know when the training session would begin and when it would end. Another feature I liked was that within each PR Zone, I had a new and defined goal. This pushed me to perform better with every workout. Before discovering EDT, I tried several methods and routines that were either extremely time-consuming, boring, and ineffective, or they were so demanding and intense that post-workout rendered me immobile! Once I started EDT workouts, I was amazed at the results even after the first workout. I was not completely exhausted, but I knew *that I had had a great workout. Working opposite muscle groups made sense to me, but it wasn't until the first couple of weeks of following the EDT protocol that I began noticing that the imbalances in my core strength were being corrected! I could literally feel my overall core body strength increasing!*

"After my first 6 weeks using EDT, almost everyone that I interfaced with each day asked me what I was doing differently. Most people knew that I was a gym rat, but the changes in my body composition aroused curiosity. The cool thing was that I was now ending my workout while most people were still warming up. After completing 16 weeks of intense EDT training for the EDT fat-loss contest, I had lost a total of 24 pounds of fat, and my body fat had dropped 8 percent! The results amazed even me! The EDT method is a motivational tool in itself. Knowing your target (from your last performance) and knowing that you have a 15-minute time zone in which to meet that goal is like an injection of energy. You have to try EDT to appreciate how effective it can be in changing your

body composition and improving your strength. I will continue to incorporate the EDT philosophy in my routine every time I step into the gym. Furthermore, Coach Staley's out-of-the-box thinking on this routine has literally changed my life and that of many others whom I have shared it with. Thanks much!"

—RONNIE BULLINS

"Charles, I just had to send you this short note to tell you what a great weapon EDT has been in assisting me and my clients accomplish seemingly insurmountable goals. EDT has become the number one option out of my toolbox when it comes to working with my clients.

"Whether it is losing body fat, gaining muscles, or simply becoming stronger, the pure simplicity of the EDT and the PR Zones has allowed my clients to push through numerous barriers. Sometimes EDT is so simple it confuses people, because they are not used to being able to manage their training sessions, but once they understand the few basic concepts, almost everyone takes to it like a duck to water. The pride and joy of my client base are my clients who are grandparents. Now you wouldn't expect a grandparent to be training on a regular basis. Well, let me tell you something—not only are my grandparents training on a regular basis, but they are breaking PRs on a weekly basis. As a matter of fact, just last week one of them set a PR by squatting 250 pounds. How did he do it? With EDT.

"Let's just put it this way: The only possible way that EDT wouldn't work is if you were totally devoid of any competitive nature at all; and even then, it's probably a better option than most. The shift to a 'performance-based program' is the key no matter what the goal. I guess what it really gets down to is if I had only one protocol to use for the rest of my career, it would be EDT!"

—TROY M. ANDERSON
Strength and conditioning coach, Tempe, Arizona

"Charles Staley's EDT is the most foolproof method of building muscle I have ever come across. And it is not the fake muscles of a pump artist; EDT muscles are as strong as they look."

—PAVEL TSATSOULINE
Author of *Power to the People!* and *The Russian Kettlebell Challenge*

"Having had some late-July overtraining issues, I took Saturday off from the gym. I did some hill work on my treadmill on Sunday. Monday was scheduled as lower-body day, and boy, I couldn't wait to get to the gym!

"On my July workout, I was to use a certain weight on the squat for the first 2 weeks. That weight

was to increase for the 3rd and 4th weeks. Being that there are 5 weeks in July, I opted to raise the weight on today's squats. I did 8 sets of 6 reps at 95 pounds (weight includes bar) and was thrilled*!*

"Back in January when I tested my 1 rep max, my 1RM on the squat was 95 pounds. If this isn't progress, I don't know what is!"

—ALICIA HATCH
Houston, Texas

"I started doing some regular cardio workouts this week, and I was amazed at how 'in shape' I am. After doing only EDT weight workouts for the last 2 months, I breezed through my first week's interval sprints, and I'm looking forward to doing more!! Amazing, isn't it!"

—ERIC LIVINGSTON
Dallas, Texas

"Charles, I just wanted to give a word out about how EDT has changed the way I train forever. It has made such a profound change in the way I think about my training that words really can't do it justice. It really epitomizes fatigue management. For example, in a 15-minute PR Zone, my only goal is to beat the total number of repetitions I had performed in the same workout before. From that vantage point, it gets my competitive juices flowing. It's me now versus me last time. No excuses—just time to step to the plate and beat what I had done. Therefore, EDT is obviously a training protocol that is extremely motivational, to say the very least.

"Since I started implementing it in my training, my martial arts performance has improved, because in my individual case, EDT helped me put on muscle, while also losing body fat, with virtually no change in my diet. I will grant that I tend to eat clean anyway, but EDT helped me put on lean muscle while shedding body fat, not just what I like to call junk muscle by stuffing my face every chance I get. In that type of scenario, I'm gaining fat and muscle. For a martial artist whose emphasis is on maintaining large amounts of relative strength, that does not bode well. There were times when my family members had asked me if I had been using steroids! Even though they know I never would, the results in my case were that profound to them, apparently.

"Because I see myself every day, it was hard to tell at first. However, then my shoulders started to appear broader, and then my abs started to really show. The ultimate way that I knew it started to have an effect is because the scale does not lie. I gained weight with these effects as well.

"One of my all-time favorite exercises is the one-arm kettlebell snatch, which will work just about as many muscles in the body that a single exercise possibly can. I used to do it for 3 sets of 10 or 5 sets of 10. Now, when I do it EDT style, I'll start out doing as many sets of 5 as possible with a weight that I can

perform 10 times maximally. I'll start out doing a set of 5 with one hand and then switch to the other. Within minutes, I am really sweating. However, I keep telling myself that I have to beat my previous result. At this stage of my training, I can tell you that I have snatched the 2-pound kettlebell, which weighs approximately 71 pounds, 154 times in just under 15 minutes. I had the blood-blistered battle scars to prove it.

"I strongly recommend everyone to incorporate EDT in their training repertoire. I even have my clients doing it, and as I count down the time, I really see them pushing to beat their previous numbers! One of the many reasons it is such a powerful training tool is because it is an objectively verifiable means of displaying improvement in one's training. Once again, I strongly urge anyone serious about training to use EDT and reap the rewards."

—NICK RADONJIC
Chicago

PART ONE

OUT WITH THE OLD, IN WITH THE NEW

CHAPTER ONE

WHY WEIGHT TRAINING WORKS

IF YOU'VE COME TO THE REALIZATION THAT RESISTANCE TRAINING IS more effective than aerobic exercise for the purposes of becoming lean, strong, and functional, your instincts have served you well. Both scientific research and "in the trenches" experience confirm that brief, high-intensity exercise burns calories, builds muscle, elevates metabolism, and improves overall athleticism more efficiently and effectively than lower-intensity forms of physical activity.

Although this book focuses primarily on resistance training, keep in mind that almost any activity, when performed in an anaerobic manner, will deliver similar results. So if you're a cycling fanatic, you'll find that multiple short, high-intensity sprints will deliver better results than a long-duration, "steady-state" ride. Let's briefly examine some of the physiological mechanisms behind the extraordinary effectiveness of intense exercise.

THE "EPOC" PHENOMENON

EPOC (or excess postexercise oxygen consumption) is basically a measure of how much energy (read: calories) is consumed after the exercise session is finished. You'll often hear novice exercisers complain about how few calories they burned during a 20-minute stint on the Stairmaster, but the fact is, you don't really burn a lot of calories during any type of exercise—it's what happens afterward that really matters.

One published study by R. Bahr, performed at the department of physiology at the National Institute of Occupational Health in Oslo, Norway, demonstrated that low-intensity exercise (defined as 65 percent of maximum heart rate for less than 1 hour) led to a total EPOC of only 5 calories. On the other hand, intensive exercise—where heart rate was above 85 percent of maximum—led to EPOC values up to 180 calories.

Another investigation showed that resistance training can lead to a 4 to 7 percent increase in metabolic rate over a 24-hour period. That might not sound like much, but consider that for a person with a 2,000-calorie-per-day metabolic rate, this equates to an extra 80 to 140 calories burned after every weight-training session. If this same person weight-trains 4 days per week, he can expect an additional 320 to 560 calories burned per week.

In addition to the metabolic-increase effects of strength training, consider the metabolic effects of the additional muscle you'll gain. Every pound of muscle you gain increases your daily metabolic rate by 30 to 40 calories per day—every day. Once again, these numbers may not initially seem significant. However, let's take a wider view for a moment: If you add 5 pounds of new muscle to your body—which is very easy to accomplish in 8 to 12 weeks, especially for beginners—that new muscle will increase your metabolism by 150 to 200 calories per day, or 1,050 to 1,400 calories per week!

Additionally, there's an interesting synergy that occurs with new muscle growth through resistance exercise: Every time you perform a strength-training workout, you achieve a certain EPOC, which is based on how much muscle you currently have—the more muscle you have, the higher your EPOC will be for any given workout. You're also gradually building more muscle, which leads not only to greater and greater EPOC but to an even faster metabolism, helping you to burn excess body fat. In other words, each success builds upon the last, and the result is faster and faster metabolism. No wonder so many people get hooked on weight training!

STRENGTH TRAINING AND THE LADDER EFFECT

There is a list of distinct motor qualities that are enhanced by exercise. These include increases in lean muscle mass, loss of body fat (these two are really one in the same and are often collectively referred to as "improvements in body composition"), improved maximal strength, speed strength, strength endurance, and aerobic endurance.

These motor qualities can be "ranked" in terms of their relative intensity. The highest level is maximal strength, which involves the greatest possible tension that a muscle can develop. The level below that represents explosive strength, followed by starting strength, anaerobic endurance, and finally, aerobic endurance.

People often want to see improvement in many or all of these areas at once. Unfortunately, they end up wasting a lot of time and energy spending equivalent time working to improve their performance in each area individually. However, the truth is that you can work on improving your performance in all of these areas simultaneously. Imagine, for instance, that you were to grab and then lift the "anaerobic endurance" rung of a rope ladder. You'd find that the aerobic endurance rung would be lifted as well, while the rungs above the anaerobic endurance rung would be undisturbed. Similarly, if you lifted the starting strength rung, only the anaerobic endurance and the aerobic endurance rungs would be affected. Finally, if you lifted the maximal strength rung of the ladder, all of the rungs below it would be dragged along with it. In a nutshell, if you're after maximum efficiency, you're better off working to improve on one of the

THE TABATA PROTOCOL

One important benefit of anaerobic training over aerobic exercise is that when you train anaerobically, you also improve aerobic fitness simultaneously, but the reverse of that doesn't hold true.

Some of the most interesting research on the subject in the past several years was performed by Izumi Tabata, PhD, at the National Institute of Fitness and Sport in Tokyo, Japan.

Tabata conducted a 6-week study in which one group of subjects (the control group) rode an exercise bike at 70 percent of VO_2 max (aerobic capacity) 5 days a week for 60 minutes per workout. The experimental group cycled at 170 percent of VO_2 max for eight 20-second bouts with 10-second rest intervals.

The control group improved their aerobic fitness by 10 percent but had no improvement in anaerobic fitness. The experimental group, however, not only improved their anaerobic capacity by 28 percent but also improved their aerobic fitness by 14 percent!

So the beauty of anaerobic training, aside from its muscle-building characteristics, is its ability to kill two birds with one stone.

And needless to say, there is a price to pay—in hard work, in time, and in effort—but here's concrete evidence that you can become significantly fitter in 20 minutes a week using anaerobic intervals than you can in 5 hours a week using aerobics.

areas at the top of the ladder. Working to improve one of these areas involves more-intensive training. That's because when you work at a high level, all other areas below it are improved at the same time. The reverse is not true, however (see "The Tabata Protocol," on page 5, for a closer look at this phenomenon). By simply working on aerobic endurance, you're not really improving your maximal strength. Working at the top of the ladder is the only way to enhance total-body motor skills.

"LIFE IS NOT AEROBIC"

This phrase was one of the favorite one-liners of Fred Hatfield, PhD, during his certification seminars for the International Sports Sciences Association (ISSA). Dr. Hatfield is a former world champion in the sport of powerlifting and the first man to officially squat 1,000 pounds in competition. Whenever Dr. Hatfield offers this mantra to audiences of personal trainers and aerobics instructors, it has the same shock value as if he'd said that the world was flat. But Dr. Hatfield is right: A true aerobic state rarely (if ever) occurs in real life. Only prolonged, steady-state exercise at moderate intensity fits the definition. It's truly a rare and artificial condition.

But doesn't aerobic exercise burn more fat?

Let's do some myth busting here: If aerobic exercise is superior to anaerobic exercise on any level, it isn't because it burns more fat. Let's take a closer look.

Aerobic and anaerobic forms of exercise both derive energy from glycogen (the body's storage form of sugar) and fats (which can come from free fatty acids in the bloodstream and/or from stored body fat deposits). Now, it is true that aerobic exercise takes more of its energy from fats than sugars (as opposed to anaerobic exercise, which is fueled more by sugars). But that's only part of the equation. As it turns out, although aerobic exercise uses fats as a primary fuel source, the problem is that it also burns far less total energy than anaerobic exercise does. So it's a wash, as they say.

SO WHY DO MOST PEOPLE STILL GRAVITATE TOWARD AEROBIC EXERCISE?

When it comes to exercise, people are polarized by pain. In other words, beginners try to avoid pain, but more experienced exercisers usually end up seeking pain.

I alluded to this phenomenon in the introduction of this book, but in essence people tend to assess the value of a workout according to how much fatigue (and by fatigue, I mean pain and soreness) it causes. Just look at the word *workout*. In eastern European countries, workouts are called "sessions" or "lessons." But in the West, we tend to focus on the difficulty inherent in the term, rather than the results, which are enhanced performance and motor skills.

And make no doubt about it; our language affects our thinking, which in turn affects our actions. Most people still cling to aerobic exercise because it hurts, it takes a long time to complete, and you sweat. It's work.

AEROBIC VERSUS ANAEROBIC EXERCISE

Most people know that the term *aerobic* means "with oxygen," but relatively few people can articulate the difference between aerobic and anaerobic forms of exercise. Here's a simple explanation.

Intensive exercise produces a waste product called lactic acid (LA)—you've experienced it before when your muscles burned in agony during a very intense workout. When you stop, the burn recedes almost immediately. That burning sensation is caused by LA.

During anaerobic exercise—weight training, sprinting, and similar intense, short-duration drills—the lactic acid (lactate) levels will reach a point called the lactate threshold (LT), where you're forced to either stop or slow down until the LA burn diminishes enough for you to continue your effort. The lactate threshold is the exertion level beyond which your body can no longer produce energy aerobically. Additional intense work means your body can't deal with the resulting lactate buildup, which is marked by muscle fatigue, pain, and shallow, rapid breathing. (LT was formerly called anaerobic threshold, but this designation is now dated. In scientific papers it's sometimes referred to as onset of blood lactate accumulation.)

Aerobic exercise on the other hand, occurs *below* the lactate threshold. You're still producing LA but at levels low enough to permit long-term, continuous activity.

These definitions reveal that any activity can be either aerobic or anaerobic, depending on the pace and duration. For example, although I'll often refer to resistance training as an anaerobic form of exercise in this book, it can actually be a form of aerobic exercise, if the exerciser uses very light weights, uses high repetitions, and takes only minimal rests between sets.

It's also important to realize that most activities are fueled by both aerobic and anaerobic processes, so when we refer to an activity's being aerobic (for example), what we really mean is that the activity is primarily or mostly aerobic in nature.

I suspect that our fondness for hard work in the gym reflects a desire to feel a sense of completion—if not at work, then in the gym. And soreness, for example, is a 24/7 concrete reminder that you worked hard and got something done.

In almost everything we do, quantity seems to trump quality. For example, if you had a hard day at the office, many people might say, "Man, I put in 10 hours at work yesterday. What a day!" (reflecting quantity). But for some reason, we'd be less likely to say, "Wow, I really employed a high percentage of my abilities at work today!" (reflecting quality).

THE MANY FACES OF STRENGTH

Without strength, no movement is possible.

That's a simple statement, but it's true. All other motor skills—including endurance, flexibility, coordination, balance, and agility—are simply modifiers of the core motor ability, and that's strength. Given the critical importance of this fitness quality, it's worth a closer look. Far from a single entity, strength is actually a family of qualities. The primary players include:

Maximal strength: Defined as the most force you can generate for a single all-out effort, regardless of time or body weight. If you've ever worked up to the heaviest squat or bench press you can possibly lift, you've tested your maximal strength.

Relative strength: The most force you can generate relative to your body weight for a single all-out effort. Think of this as your "pound for pound" strength. If you and your training partner can deadlift 300 pounds, you both have the same level of maximal strength. However, if you weigh less than your buddy, you've got greater relative strength.

Speed strength: Also called "power," speed strength is the most force you can generate relative to time. Think of speed strength as maximal strength divided by time. If your training partner can deadlift that 300-pound barbell in 1.8 seconds and you can lift it in 2.1 seconds, he has a greater degree of speed strength than you do, at least with respect to the deadlift exercise.

Anaerobic strength: Your ability to perform repeated muscular contractions in activities conducted above the lactate threshold. This quality is critical to sprint performances between the 100-meter and 800-meter distances in track and field.

Aerobic strength: Your ability to perform repeated muscular contractions in activities conducted under the lactate threshold. This quality is critical to running performances at distances greater than 800 meters in track and field.

My experiences as a martial arts instructor and competitor taught me a great deal about human nature with respect to the quality-quantity conundrum. I've found that most instructors stress repetition to the virtual exclusion of quality. As a competitor, I'd attend classes where we'd perform many hundreds of kicks, yet because of extreme fatigue, most of those kicks were well below 50 percent of my true technical capabilities in a fresh state. But if you hung in there, you'd receive praise for your internal fortitude. Despite this, most of these instructors loved to recite the mantras "Practice makes perfect" and "One perfect punch is better than 1,000 poorly executed punches." Yet in practice, the disconnect was starkly obvious. I never received praise for performing a single move with perfect technique!

THE MASTER PRINCIPLE: QUALITY BEFORE QUANTITY

In my practice as a sports performance coach, I rely on tested principles that have evolved over many years of work with clients. The first of these principles is that in any movement, quality must take precedence over quantity. With resistance training in particular, the first objective is to achieve an efficient, safe, pain-free "grooved" motor pattern or performance. Every rep looks exactly the same—almost like you're a machine instead of a living being. Once this has been achieved, we seek the ability to produce momentary high levels of force during the movement pattern. Only when these foundational goals are met do we seek the ability to perform greater amounts of total work (volume) with that movement or exercise. Should you choose to ignore my advice in this paragraph, you'll pay the price in the form of less dramatic results and more injuries. If, however, you consistently live and die by this principle, you'll be rewarded by many years of productive, injury-free training.

UNDERSTANDING QUALITY VERSUS QUANTITY

In resistance training, quality or intensity is normally expressed as a percentage of 1RM (single repetition maximum, or 1 rep max). For example, let's assume that your best military press for 1 rep (or your 1RM) is 190 pounds. Today you lifted 152 pounds for 8 sets of 3 repetitions on the military press. Since 152 pounds is 80 percent of 190, your intensity for that workout would be calculated as 80 percent of maximum.

In the same workout, the quantity of military presses you performed would be expressed as the total amount of weight lifted on that exercise. In this example, 190 multiplied by 24 repetitions equals 4,560 pounds—this is your training quantity, or volume, for that exercise for that day.

An important thing to note is that despite its ease of use, the above definition of quality is somewhat flawed. In truth, the training effect you experience from lifting a weight is a product not only of the weight itself but also of how fast that weight is lifted. Think of it this way: If I placed a 10-pound plate on your foot, you wouldn't feel any pain at all. However, if I dropped that plate on your foot from a height of 6 feet, you'd experience plenty of pain! In both cases, the weight is the same, but it's the speed that makes the deciding difference. The same principle applies in resistance training: The faster you move any given weight, the more tension your muscles will experience.

CHAPTER TWO

END A LIFETIME OF CONFUSION IN 15 MINUTES

DESPITE WEIGHT TRAINING'S RELIABLE, DOCUMENTED ABILITY TO produce a wide spectrum of beneficial results, many people, especially novice lifters, find themselves confused over the almost endless array of techniques, methods, and philosophies they're exposed to in books, magazine articles, and the advice of various experts. In fact, if you've done any amount of reading on the subject, you'll find that most top training experts seem to contradict one another (and sometimes even themselves!) in their articles and books.

Virtually every aspect of weight training—including training frequency, exercise selection, lifting speed, the ideal number of sets and/or reps per exercise, the optimal number of exercises per session, proper exercise technique, optimal rest between sets, and load selection—is the subject of intense debate among exercise scientists and coaches working in the trenches. All of this intense debate can cause something I like to call "paralysis by analysis"—a state of confusion that prevents you from doing anything.

Now, if you're relatively new to weight training, you're in luck—this book will save you years of needless frustration. On the other hand, if you're an experienced gym rat and you can relate to the paralysis by analysis I just referred to, here's the good news (and you probably already realize this on some level): Weight training usually delivers great results regardless of how you manage the variables described earlier. In fact, it's incredibly fascinating—and to some people perplexing—to learn how the training programs of successful athletes and bodybuilders have differed over the years. Some top bodybuilders rely almost exclusively on variable resistance machines, while others concentrate mainly on free weights. Many athletes swear by 1 set per exercise per session, while others insist upon many (between 5 and 10) sets per exercise. Traditionally, elite-level powerlifters have performed the three competitive lifts (the squat, the bench press, and the deadlift) with maximum or nearly maximum weights in their workouts. Despite the proven success of this method, a newer, equally successful training strategy advocates the use of moderate weights on the competitive lifts combined with heavier weights on "assistance exercises."

One of the most recent contributions to the arena of exercise confusion is called "functional training." With its roots in the fields of physical therapy and rehabilitation, functional training features exercises performed on various devices—such as exercise balls, foam rollers, and "wobble boards"—that are designed to create a more challenging environment for the purpose of in-

FUNCTIONAL-TRAINING FOLLIES

If you're a longtime gym rat, you've no doubt noticed the proliferation of what trainers call functional training (or FT). Typically this involves the use of stability balls and various other implements or techniques designed to create an "unstable" exercise experience for the neuromuscular system. Proponents of FT insist that their methods provide a much-needed training effect for the "stabilizer" muscles.

Like almost everything else in life, there is a grain of truth to this idea—the problem is in the casual, across-the-board implementation of FT by trainers and coaches. While it is true that exercising on an unstable surface (as when you perform an abdominal crunch while seated on a stability ball) or in an unstable manner (as when you perform a barbell curl while standing on one foot) may provide a novel stimulus for your muscles, in more cases than not the instability does more harm than good by compromising the safety of the exercise—you can lose your balance—and/or by limiting the amount of weight you could otherwise use, thereby minimizing the tension experienced by the muscles.

For the most part, I suggest leaving stability balls and wobble boards to the physical therapists and performing your weight-training movements in a stable environment.

volving more of the smaller and more deeply located "stabilizer" muscles. Functional-training advocates purport that greater stabilizer involvement is the key to enhanced performance and overall training results. And they're right—sometimes.

THE FIVE PILLARS OF SUCCESSFUL WEIGHT TRAINING

I've studied this perplexing mess of exercise confusion with great interest for many years and arrived at five "universal conclusions" that will help you sort your way through the information overload.

1. There is no best way. Despite the human mind's preference for quick, no-brainer answers, when it comes to weight training, there simply is no one best way. In fact, if there were a best way, it probably would have been discovered many years ago, thus alleviating the need for further discussion. As I mentioned earlier, both history and practical experience confirm that many approaches can and do work in the proper context. A useful analogy is to think of various weight-training methods, techniques, and philosophies as tools in a toolbox. Just as we can't say there is a best tool without knowing the intended use, there is no one best exercise, method, or weight-training philosophy. Many ways can and do work, if they are matched to the appropriate context and outcome.

2. Everything works. At least temporarily, that is. If you're a total newbie to weight training, the moment you pick up a dumbbell, your muscles are already experiencing a higher degree of physical stress than they're used to. As a result of this stress, these muscles will experience a training effect of some sort, albeit slight.

3. Nothing works forever. I can still recall the first time I performed barbell squats. I was only 17 years old, and I squatted 3 sets of 10 reps with 75 pounds. The soreness and debilitation that resulted from that workout was both surprising and astounding. Later that evening, my legs seemed to have a mind of their own as they trembled and spasmed while I attempted to walk from the couch to the office in the next room! Today, at age 45, I can easily squat 3 × 10, with three times that much weight, with little or no soreness. It's easy to understand why. After almost 30 years of squats, my strength levels and familiarity with the squat have increased considerably, so now I require a significantly greater challenge to invoke the same kind of soreness that I experienced as a newbie to the squat almost 30 years ago. Put simply, our neuromuscular systems react with alarm to unfamiliar physical challenges. Familiar challenges result in little more than a yawn, metaphorically speaking. This fact speaks to the need for regular changes in your exercise program if continued progress is to be expected.

4. Fitness results from greater performances, not greater pain. When it comes to weight training, most people tend to be "polarized by pain." As I said in Chapter One, beginners try to avoid it at all costs, while experienced trainees actually tend to seek pain. In fact, the more experienced you are, the more you'll tend to assume that pain (and by pain, I mean soreness, tightness, fatigue, and/or the "burn" that often accompanies hard training) is the best way to assess the value of a workout. I'll discuss this fallacy in more depth in the next chapter, but for now suffice it to say that "fatigue seeking" is not the most efficient path to your goals.

5. Don't expect Mother Nature to cooperate. Nature is conservative. She thinks your purpose on this planet is to live long enough to reproduce—nothing more, nothing less. Except for the lucky few, most of us need to convince Mother Nature that more muscle is necessary for survival. That means intense workouts. How intense? More intense than what you're used to.

Q&A

Q: *I love Escalating Density Training, but after my first two workouts, I'm so sore, I can barely dress myself in the morning! Should I wait for the soreness to go away before I do the next workout?*

A: Yes. For the sake of providing clear direction, the programs in this book feature a Monday–Wednesday–Friday pattern. But don't be afraid to make modifications to the schedule when necessary. My rule of thumb regarding soreness is that you should not resume training until you've had at least one full day of no soreness for the muscles in question. So if you're still sore on Wednesday from the previous workout, postpone the session until the soreness has dissipated. Over time, your body will adjust to the program, and you won't need to postpone workouts due to soreness. Remember that soreness is an indicator that your muscles are in a state of repair—it's important to allow the repair process to be completed before you expose the muscle to additional stress.

With these universal truths in mind, I'd also like to remind you that all forms of self-development require some degree of patience as you work your way through the learning curve. Weight training is no different. Remember also that mastery requires a tolerance for "not knowing"—even though I'm considered a leader in the field of human performance and fitness, I'd be willing to bet that I have many more questions about training than you do!

The journey need not be arduous, however, and the rewards you'll experience will exceed all of your expectations. After all, when I performed that first squat workout all those years ago, who could have known that weight training would come to occupy such an important place in my life? I guess I could say that I've truly been bitten by the bug, and I'm betting that by the time you finish this book, you will be, too.

CHAPTER THREE

THE FOUR COMMANDMENTS OF TRAINING FOR OPTIMAL RESULTS

IN ANY FIELD OF ENDEAVOR, PRINCIPLES FORM THE FOUNDATION OF both knowledge and practice.

Whenever you find yourself confused or have a question about resistance training, the principles described in this chapter will provide the answer. The following four principles can be viewed as "commandments," because if your training program ignores even one of them, it will be doomed to failure. Programs that abide by all four of these principles will be, by definition, successful programs.

COMMANDMENT ONE: THE PRINCIPLE OF PROGRESSIVE OVERLOAD

This is the "mother" principle of weight training, the bedrock upon which all other principles rest. If your resistance-training program doesn't abide by this principle, it isn't really resistance training.

As you'll see when we begin to explore Escalating Density Training in more detail, the goal of each PR Zone is to gradually perform more and more total repetitions in the same time period or, in other words, to gradually increase or escalate the density of the workout each time you repeat it. This unique method of applying the progressive overload principle leads to rapid improvements in lean mass gain, local muscle endurance, work capacity, and body fat reduction.

Milo of Crotona

You may have heard of the story of Milo. The entire field of resistance training is founded on and explained by this simple story. Basically, Milo was a young man who dedicated his life to becoming stronger. Interestingly, he was a lot smarter than many of today's fitness trainers and strength coaches, at least when it came to getting stronger. Milo took a very young calf and lifted it onto his shoulders once a day, every day. As the calf grew, Milo found himself lifting a gradually heavier load every day, until eventually he could lift a full-grown steer.

Milo's little experiment exploited the fact that the human body, like any living system, is adaptable. This means that it can change itself in order to cope with new stresses that it might encounter. If you lie out in the sun, you'll get a tan (or a sunburn if you lie out too long). If you use a wrench every day, you'll get calluses (or blisters, if you do too much too soon). Similarly, if you contract your muscles against a greater resistance than they are used to, they'll grow bigger and/or stronger.

That's the principle of progressive overload in a nutshell: Simply expose your body to progressively greater and greater challenges, and it will adapt accordingly. In resistance training, there are a number of ways you can employ the overload principle, and all of them can, and do, work. They include lifting a larger weight, lifting the same weight for more reps or for more sets, lifting a weight over a greater range of motion, lifting the weight slower or faster (either can be a form of overload, believe it or not), and lifting a weight in an unaccustomed manner (for example, performing an ab crunch on a Swiss ball instead of from the floor).

Note: Despite the popularity of calisthenic exercises, such as situps, pushups, and the like, the problem is that the resistance—your own body weight—is difficult to increase as your strength levels improve. Although calisthenics can be used during the warmup and for light training days, they tend to be a poor choice for developing muscle and strength.

Understanding the Concept of Training Load

There are three principle components of what is called "the training load" that you can manipulate over the course of a training cycle—intensity, volume, and density. Let's briefly examine each.

HOW FAST SHOULD YOU LIFT THE WEIGHT?

The phrase "Lift the weight slowly and under control" is terribly overused by fitness trainers today—whenever I hear it, my eyes sort of glaze over, and I'm sure yours do, too.

Truthfully, this advice is a disservice in many ways, because it somehow leads many people to think that slowness actually defines good technique. It doesn't!

Lifting speed (often called "tempo") is a source of endless and often heated debate among exercise scientists and weight-lifting buffs. On one end of the spectrum are devotees of the "super-slow" philosophy, which claims that very slow lifting (up to 30 seconds per repetition) is the key to safe progress. On the other end of the debate are Olympic weight lifters and power-lifting specialists who emphasize explosive lifting techniques for the most-rapid progress.

Here are my thoughts on the issue. The faster you lift a given weight, the more tension your muscles and supporting tissues experience. This can be good or bad, depending on your orthopedic history and training status—if the tension is greater than your body's ability to withstand it, you'll end up injured. However, your musculoskeletal system needs a certain minimal amount of tension if a training effect is to be expected. The key is to find the "sweet spot"—enough tension to provoke a training response, but not so much as to cause injury.

$$\text{weight} \times \text{speed} = \text{tension}$$

Whenever you lift a weight, there are two components that together produce tension across the muscles, tendons, and ligaments: the weight, and the speed used to lift the weight. Recall the analogy from Chapter One: If I placed a 10-pound weight on your foot, it wouldn't hurt. But if I dropped that weight from a height of 6 feet, it *would* most certainly hurt. In both cases, the weight is the same. The dramatically different result is a function of the speed of impact.

My philosophy favors doing *more with less.* I'd rather use a moderate weight and create higher tensions by applying more speed than use very heavy weights and less speed. This approach is safer, because it gives you a buffer—you can instantly regulate tension by varying the speed.

One other point of interest: The design of the neuromuscular system is most suited to accelerative lifting. If you watch people carefully in various situations, you'll notice that whenever there is an option to accelerate a load, people will take that option. On stairclimbing machines, people will tend to step in a bouncy, choppy manner.

As you implement the EDT training programs in this book, I encourage you to lower weights at a comfortable, controllable speed and lift them aggressively—with speed—maintaining proper form and posture throughout.

INTENSITY

This simply means the absolute difficulty of the resistance you're using. You can also think of it as the "quality" of the load. As I mentioned earlier, in resistance training, intensity is traditionally expressed as a percentage of 1RM (your single repetition maximum, or 1 rep max). Your 1RM is defined as the most weight you can lift for 1 rep (but not 2). So, for example, if you can squat 200 pounds for 1 rep and today you've decided to lift 160 pounds for 5 sets of 5 reps, you'd be using 80 percent of your current 1RM for that exercise. If next week you decide you're going to attempt to use 170 pounds for the same sets and reps, you'd be using 85 percent of 1RM.

One point I'd like to make right away is that basing your training weights on 1RMs has benefits as well as drawbacks. It seems very precise and methodical; however, there is a problem—most people's 1RMs are likely to vary quite a bit over the course of a day, a week, or a month. Another problem is that testing your 1RM strength is potentially dangerous, especially for beginners, who may lack the technical precision and experience to handle maximum weights.

Fortunately, Escalating Density Training (EDT) ensures that you'll be respecting the overload principle during all of your weight-training sessions: All sets and reps are performed in predetermined 15-minute time periods called PR Zones. During each PR Zone, you'll perform two "antagonistic" exercises (more on this later), with the aim of completing as many total reps as possible for each exercise, using approximately 10RM weights—that is, weights that can be lifted 10 (but not 11) times. Whenever you're able to improve upon your total number of reps by a certain percentage, you'll have "earned" the right to use more weight the next time around.

Q&A

Q: *How did you arrive at 15 minutes for PR Zones? Can I use shorter or longer PR Zones?*

A: We arrived at 15 minutes through trial and error. This isn't to say that 10- or 20-minute PR Zones can't be used, however. For example, people who've never weight-trained—or who haven't done so in a long time—will do just fine with 10-minute PR Zones for the first 3 or 4 weeks. So don't be afraid to get creative with EDT. As long as the basic underlying principles are maintained, you can modify the system to suit your own individual needs.

Q&A

Q: *Should the total volume of each exercise within a PR Zone be the same? In other words, if I were to add up the total weight lifted for each exercise, should it be the same?*

A: No. While for any given PR Zone you should perform the same number of total reps for each exercise, the volume—the weight multiplied by total reps—won't necessarily be the same. For example, if you're performing chins and triceps pushdowns, the volume for chins will be much greater than the pushdown volume (since the weight used for chins will be your entire body weight).

As you might expect, however, there are a few additional factors to consider.

- **New challenges to your body should be gradually progressive. If you can currently curl 95 pounds for 3 sets of 12 repetitions, for example, and you perform this workout once every 5 days, you shouldn't try to increase the load or the reps per set by more than maybe 5 percent per workout—doing so is unnecessary and invites the possibility of injury.**

- **Your progress (which for most translates to strength increases rather than additional muscle gain) won't continue at the same rate throughout your lifting career. Progress will be fast at the beginning and will gradually slow down as you become more experienced. It's not unusual for a beginner to double his strength in a handful of months, but once you've been in the game for several years, you'll be lucky to experience even a tenth of that progress in the same time frame. That's great news for beginners, and for you advanced lifters, it just means you'll need to get a bit sneakier to coax a bit more from your body.**

- **As you might expect, if you reduce your training intensity and/or volume, or if you remove it altogether, your body's adaptations will eventually disappear. This is sometimes called the "principle of reversibility." Put another way, "Use it or lose it." In essence, if you want to be stronger and more muscular, you've got to give your body a damned good reason (in the form of hard training backed up by smart nutritional practices). Your body wants to be only as big and strong as it needs to be, and not one bit more.**

VOLUME

Training volume simply refers to the amount of work that you perform in a given time period. You could, for example, track your volume for a single workout or for one week or for a month's worth of training. Whereas intensity is the quality of your training, volume is the quantity. Successful resistance training requires progressive increases in both intensity and volume at one point or another but rarely at the same time. If your training is high quality, it won't be high quantity, and vice versa. Think of it this way: You can't run a marathon at 100-meter-sprint speed, nor can you perform 8 reps with your 1RM. So, as a general rule, the heavier the load, the less total work you'll perform with it.

DENSITY

Density is a measure of the work-to-rest ratio of any specified period of time. Therefore, one could refer to the density of a set, a workout, or even a training cycle. Density is normally expressed as a percentage of the total training unit. For example, if you were to perform 3 sets of 10 chins, where each repetition took 3 seconds to complete and you rested 3 minutes between sets, you would quickly see that the total training duration was 8.5 minutes, and the "work" portion of that workout was 1.5 minutes. Thus, the density of this particular workout would be 17.6 percent.

COMMANDMENT TWO: THE PRINCIPLE OF SPECIFICITY

Specificity simply means that a specific type of training will yield a specific result. There are a lot of applications of this principle—some are obvious; some are a bit subtler. Here are a few of the more obvious examples of the specificity principle in action.

- If you want bigger arms, you need to focus on exercises for the biceps and triceps.
- If you want to bench-press more, you need to concentrate on that specific exercise.
- If you want to improve your tennis serve, you'll need to spend most of your time working on tennis serves.

Now a less obvious example of the specificity principle: Some muscles (the hamstrings are an example) are composed of primarily fast-twitch muscle fibers (a type of muscle tissue that is capable of great force generation but poor endurance capacity). Therefore, the principle of specificity would suggest that you train these muscles using heavy weight and/or maximum speed, since fast-twitch fibers are more responsive to high-tension stresses.

COMMANDMENT THREE: THE PRINCIPLE OF VARIATION

The training methods and techniques you use must be periodically changed or your body will reduce its adaptive response. In fact, every time you repeat a particular exercise or training method, you'll derive less benefit from it than you did the previous time. The more familiar your body becomes with a particular type of stress, the less it reacts. Bottom line: Your progress stagnates.

Variation is more important for advanced trainees than it is for beginners, for at least two reasons. First, everything a beginner does in the gym is new. For the first several months, the beginner's training experience is rife with novelty and variation. Therefore, the body is in a constant state of adaptation, trying to get stronger and more muscular to meet myriad physical demands. Advanced athletes have a harder path, however: Their bodies have already experienced a great deal of variety. Paradoxically, the answer for these trainees is to seek ever newer and fresher challenges, which is why experienced athletes are well known for all sorts of experimentation, some of which might seem a bit irrational at a casual glance!

Q&A

Q: *How often should I change my program?*

A: Over the years, I've found that there is no golden rule for how often you should change the cycle you're using, other than current effectiveness—if the program you're using is still working, keep using it. Generally, I recommend 8 weeks of EDT, followed by 1 week completely off, followed by 3 weeks of the 3–5 Method (described in Chapter Ten).

The second reason that advanced trainees need more variation is to maintain good orthopedic health and to avoid overuse injuries. More-experienced exercisers are, by definition, older and more prone to joint symptoms, and the best way to maintain a good level of progress is to make training as varied as possible. In this manner, physical stresses are distributed over a wide range of joint angles, body positions, velocities, and volume/intensity relationships.

Fortunately, there are an almost unlimited number of ways to introduce variety into your program, and we'll explore some of these options in more detail in the chapter on programming.

COMMANDMENT FOUR: THE PRINCIPLE OF INDIVIDUALITY

Despite the reliability of the previously discussed principles, there's another factor that must be considered when putting your training program together: Everyone's different.

If, for example, 1,000 of you perform one of the sample programs I've provided in Part Two of this book, you will all experience a slightly different result. And to complicate things, if the same 1,000 people again performed that same program 5 years from now, they'd get a whole new batch of slightly different results, because people's bodies, health statuses, and fitness levels will change over time.

Once again, think of these training principles as the four commandments of safe and effective training. Any training program or system that corresponds with these principles will ultimately be effective. However, not all training systems are equally efficient. That's where EDT comes in. Built upon the foundation of these four established training principles, EDT takes things a step further, dramatically improving efficiency by intelligently organizing exercise menus, sets, reps, and rest intervals. This combination of great effectiveness married to great efficiency is what makes EDT such a rewarding style of training.

CHAPTER FOUR

LIBERATE YOURSELF FROM CLASSIC WEIGHT TRAINING

NOW THAT WE'VE OUTLINED THE SUPERIORITY OF ANAEROBIC FORMS of exercise for the purposes of lean mass gain, fat loss, and athletic performance, it's time to introduce the Escalating Density Training (EDT) system.

EDT evolved over the course of several years of in-the-trenches experimentation, scientific research, and careful analysis of existing training systems. The EDT system also has roots in established time-management principles and practices. But the true birth of EDT occurred in March 2001, when I arrived at an arresting premise: In resistance training, the ends must dictate the means.

This realization struck me as profound, because it directly opposes the principles virtually all other systems are based on. What I began to focus my efforts on was this question: How can I organize sets, reps, rest intervals, and so forth in such a way that I can perform the most work possible in a predetermined time frame? In the process of my asking this question, a fundamental truth emerged: Work capacity is a function of managing (rather than seeking) fatigue.

This principle is a universal truth in all other fields of endeavor. It is also the hallmark of all effective people. In his excellent book *Leadership*, Rudolph Giuliani states that one of his primary objectives was to get as much done as possible in the first hour of the day, while his energy was still high. This is a strategy that I have used in my own professional life for many years, and maybe you have, too. The point is simple: Effectiveness, whether at the office, at home, or in the weight room, is primarily a function of managing resources—time and energy in particular.

DR. DELORME'S 3 × 10 METHOD

Arguably the most common set/rep format used by gym rats is the old standby, 3 sets of 10. This format originated from the work of Dr. Thomas DeLorme, an orthopedic surgeon and strength researcher at Massachusetts General Hospital during the 1940s, more than 50 years ago, and it's still popular today. DeLorme's original protocol worked like this.

Take a barbell and load it to 50 percent of your 1RM (1 rep max, or the most weight you can lift for a single repetition) and perform 10 reps with that weight. Assuming that you're performing squats and your max is 250 pounds on that exercise, you'd squat 125 pounds for 10 reps. Next, rest for about 3 minutes, load the bar to 75 percent of 1RM (187.5 pounds in this case), and perform another set of 10. Finally, rest for another 3 minutes, load the bar to your current 1RM (250 pounds in this example), and perform your third and final set of 10.

Over the years, DeLorme's original system has gradually taken on a slightly different form, and today "3 sets of 10" means lifting the same weight for all 3 sets. Now, you really can't lift a true 10RM weight for more than 1 set of 10 reps (after the first set, you'd be totally shot), so typically lifters will use perhaps a 12RM load for 3 × 10. What happens is that after the first 2 sets, fatigue accumulates to the point where the weight is actually a momentary 10RM weight for the final set. So basically, the purpose of sets 1 and 2 is to generate enough fatigue so that the final set requires a maximal effort to complete successfully.

You have probably used this routine. It was hard, and for the next few days you were sore—really sore. That soreness was confirmation that you put your work in, and it was satisfying. You became hooked.

But guess what? There's a better way. And just for the sake of illustration, let's do a crazy experiment and look at what happens when we do the exact opposite of the 3 × 10 format—namely, 10 sets of 3 repetitions.

FORCE PRODUCTION DURING 1 SET OF 10 REPS . . .

Imagine a hypothetical lifting contest between two lifters. One lifter (we'll call him Jeff) performs 3 sets of 10 with the heaviest weight he can manage (let's say it's 135 pounds), and he completes all 3 sets in 10 minutes. The other lifter, Mark, does the exact opposite—he performs 10 sets of 3 reps, also with 135 pounds, and also completes his 10 sets within 10 minutes. Here's the question—who gets the better result?

In my seminars, most people will argue, "Well, of course Jeff will get the best workout—after all, if you're only doing sets of 3 with a weight that you can lift 10 times, you're not working hard enough to get a good workout!" But let's examine the numbers. Each lifter performed 30 repetitions with 135 pounds in 10 minutes. Another way to put it is that they both lifted 4,050 pounds in 10 minutes. Put very simply, both lifters did exactly the same amount of work in the same amount of time.

You might now think that it's a trick question—Jeff and Mark obviously got the same benefit from their workouts, right?

Wrong. Since Mark, the 10 × 3 lifter, organized his workload in a way that managed fatigue, he was able to apply more force on the bar for each repetition. And that's critically important.

Let's take a look for a moment at Jeff's set of 10 reps with 135 pounds. How much force (expressed in pounds) did he exert on the 10th rep? Well, clearly, it's at least 135 pounds or he wouldn't have successfully completed the rep. And just as clearly it wasn't much more than 135 pounds, because if it was, he'd probably get an 11th rep, correct?

So, just for the sake of argument, let's say that Jeff created about 136 pounds of force on that 10th repetition.

Next question: How much force did he exert on the 9th rep? Well of course, Jeff wasn't quite as fatigued on rep 9 as he was on rep 10; therefore, he was able to produce a bit more force on the 9th rep—we'll say he produced 138 pounds of force. If we continue this pattern for the entire set, it'll look something like this:

Rep 1: 154 pounds of force

Rep 2: 152 pounds of force

Rep 3: 150 pounds of force

Rep 4: 148 pounds of force

Rep 5: 146 pounds of force

Rep 6: 144 pounds of force

Rep 7: 142 pounds of force

Rep 8: 140 pounds of force

Rep 9: 138 pounds of force

Rep 10: 136 pounds of force

Now, as you examine these numbers, don't get too hung up on whether or not they're exactly accurate—they're probably not. What is accurate, however, is the pattern. Specifically, with each rep, force output decreases, due to accumulating fatigue. And when force output goes down, so does the result of your workout.

Analyzing these numbers, we can quickly see that the average force output for this set of 10 is 145 pounds per rep. If Jeff performs 3 sets of 10 over a 10-minute time period, here are his numbers.

Bar weight: 135 pounds

Total volume: 4,050 pounds (135 multiplied by 30 reps)

Average force per rep (expressed in pounds): 145

Now let's take a look at Mark's workout. We'll assume that he has exactly the same strength as Jeff. During each set of 3, his numbers will look the same as Jeff's first 3 reps.

Rep 1: 154 pounds of force

Rep 2: 152 pounds of force

Rep 3: 150 pounds of force

Here, then, are the statistics for Mark's workout.

Bar weight: 135 pounds

Total volume: 4,050 pounds (135 multiplied by 30 reps)

Average force per rep (expressed in pounds): 152

As you can see, the numbers are identical, with one exception: Mark's average force is 152 pounds (compared with Jeff's 145). This higher average force per rep will make an important impact on the results Mark gets from his workouts—the higher forces will lead to greater muscular tensions, which will in turn lead to greater strength and hypertrophy (lean mass gain). An additional benefit is that since Mark will never lift to failure—or even close to it—he won't be as reliant on a spotter for safety. His workouts will be psychologically less stressful also, which means he'll recover faster than Jeff. All in all, the benefits of this "contrarian" approach to lifting clearly outweigh the more conventional approach. True, many "fatigue seekers" just won't be able to see how less-painful workouts can be more effective, but if you can see the logic, that's all that matters.

Now, although EDT workouts don't use the 10 × 3 method per se, they do employ a number of fatigue-management tactics that lead to the same kind of improved results we've been talking about. In fact, EDT optimizes work output in the following ways.

ANTAGONISTIC PAIRINGS: Here's a common practice that completely kills most lifters' efficiency in the gym: straight sets. This refers to performing all sets of a particular exercise before moving on to the next exercise. This is the way that 90 percent of all lifters train, but it's terribly inefficient. Most exercise physiology students have studied the work of Dr. Sir Charles Scott Sherrington, a British neurophysiology researcher and winner of the Nobel Prize in 1932. The good doctor observed that when a muscle contracts to overcome a resistance, its antagonist—the muscle on the other side of the joint—must relax; otherwise, no movement can occur. To experience Sherrington's Law firsthand, grab a moderately heavy dumbbell and curl it with your right arm. As you do so, reach around and feel your right triceps—you'll find that it's totally flaccid. EDT applies this principle to resistance training by organizing workouts according to antagonistic exercise pairings. For example, a typical EDT arm session would involve working back and forth between a biceps exercise (say, barbell curls) and a triceps exercise (say, dumbbell triceps extensions). When exercises are arranged in this way, recovery between sets is accelerated—in this example, during your set of triceps extensions, the biceps will recover even faster than if you were to rest completely during sets of curls. It's a counterintuitive concept, but it works. In EDT, three types of antagonists are recognized.

- **True antagonist:** "True" antagonists are two muscles whose actions exactly oppose each other—for example, a knee flexor and a knee extensor or the pectoralis major and the latissimus dorsi.

- **Bilateral antagonist:** When using unilateral (single limb) exercises, such as dumbbell rows or lunges, the left side becomes the antagonist for the right side, and vice versa.

■ **Proximal antagonist:** In some regimens of EDT training, two distal (distantly located) muscle groups are trained together in the same PR Zone as a way to manage fatigue. For example, leg curls and incline presses can be trained during the same PR Zone.

OPTIMAL FORCE-VELOCITY RELATIONSHIP: As we discussed earlier, the speed with which you lift a weight has a telling effect on the final result. Most lifters have been taught to lift the weight "slowly and under control." This advice, when applied across the board, is flawed in two major ways. First, good control is not dependent upon lifting the weight slowly. Olympic weight lifters literally throw very heavy barbells from the floor to an overhead position, and their sport requires impeccable precision and timing. Second, lifting a weight quickly is not patently dangerous, despite the warnings of the Super Slow Exercise Guild. While it is true that lifting a weight faster places more stress on your muscles and joints, remember that stress is the primary precondition for muscular growth! Only when the stress exceeds your body's ability to withstand it does injury become a possibility.

In EDT workouts, trainees are advised to start each PR Zone by performing sets of 5 with a 10RM weight.

Select a 10RM weight. Most important, each PR Zone starts with sets of 5 with this 10RM weight—exactly the opposite of what most training systems recommend. The rationale? By selecting a moderate weight and lifting it with acceleration (see "Compensatory Acceleration Training [CAT]" on page 32), we strike a balance between force and speed that results in the highest possible motor unit recruitment and work output.

REST INTERVALS: Perhaps the most common misconception about EDT involves rests between sets. Many people assume that the idea is to move quickly back and forth between sets as they progress through each PR Zone. Not necessarily true—in fact, the true goal is to rest as much as possible between sets, as long as you still manage to improve upon your PRs. Generally, however, in any given PR Zone, rest intervals will range between 10 and 60 seconds.

THE CHRONOLOGICAL GOVERNOR (PR ZONES): Most automobiles have a "governor," which sets a limit on how fast the vehicle can be driven. This is designed to protect both you and the vehicle. EDT training uses a similar device, called the PR Zone, to limit the amount of high-intensity work you perform in an exercise session. Typically, EDT workouts feature two or three PR Zones, usually 15 minutes in duration. Note that most exercise systems provide you with a certain number of exercises, sets, and reps, and then you perform that workout, regardless of how long it takes to complete. EDT employs the opposite approach—first, you set the time limit, and then you perform as much work as possible within that time frame.

DEFINITIVE PROGRESSION TARGETS: Unlike most training systems, EDT workouts provide a specific performance goal for each PR Zone. You start the workout knowing exactly how much time you have and exactly what must be accomplished. This provides focus and clarity for each and every workout.

Most training systems pay a lot of lip service to the principle of progressive overload but provide only vague directions with regard to when you should increase the weight and by how much. EDT workouts employ what is known as the Critical Density Index (CDI). That is, whenever you can improve your PR (on any given exercise pairing) by 20 percent or more, add 5 pounds or 5 percent (whichever is less) on both exercises the next time you repeat the PR Zone. If, on the other hand, your total reps fall short of your PR for that pairing, you'll reduce your weight on the next outing. For example, let's say that your PR for a particular exercise pairing is 40 reps. When you repeat that PR Zone several days later, say you manage only 31 reps, or 77.5 percent. This is a sign that you are overtrained, which means you should reduce your training load for the next workout. The rule is that if you miss your previous PR by 20 percent or more, reduce the weight by 5 pounds or 5 percent (whichever is more) on the next workout, and start anew.

THE DISTRACTION PRINCIPLE: Many people read magazines, watch TV, listen to music, or chat away on their cell phones to take their minds off their workouts. However, I'd rather have your mind on your workouts! Nevertheless, there is an interesting phenomenon that occurs during EDT workouts—you've always got one eye on the clock and the other on your training log. There's little time to consider how tired you are, what you'll eat for lunch afterward, or any other distracting thoughts. It's very much like the airplane pilot during an emergency—he's far too busy to be nervous or scared. Every EDT workout is a self-contained competition with yourself. You're always busy breaking through your PRs from workout to workout—proof positive that you're making progress.

THE CONSCIENTIOUS PARTICIPATION PRINCIPLE: Virtually all other training systems impose themselves upon the user, who has no active input in the system. In other words, "Here's the program—now go do it." EDT, on the other hand, has "intuitive intelligence." Much like a smart bomb that knows exactly how to get to its target, EDT adjusts to you (rather than the other way around) workout by workout. This means that every workout you do becomes more effective than the one that preceded it. You'll be absolutely assured of always performing the optimal number of exercises, sets, reps, and workouts. Here's an example of what I mean.

Although I suggest starting each PR Zone by performing sets of 5 with 10RM weights, this is just a guideline. Workout by workout, each individual trainee eventually finds the best set-rep-rest strategy to permit an optimal performance. For example, people with a predominance of slow-twitch muscle fibers often find that higher reps and shorter rests result in the best performances. People who are "fast twitchers" do just the opposite. A number of individual factors determine optimal exercise performance for each person, and EDT provides the flexibility to capitalize on individual talents and predilections. Consider this analogy: Water, being fluid and adaptable, always takes the shape of its container. Other systems are more like ice, however—they fit only if you're the right size container!

COMPENSATORY ACCELERATION TRAINING (CAT): Coined by Fred Hatfield, PhD, the first man to officially squat 1,000 pounds in competition, compensatory acceleration training is a way to optimize the training effect of any given weight load. Now, the personal trainer down at your local spa will tell you that fast lifting reduces the load on the muscle, since "momentum is lifting the weight." Although it is true that momentum does become a factor when you add speed to a lift, CAT solves the problem in a uniquely simple way: As momentum begins to accumulate, you compensate for that momentum by accelerating the weight even more. Basically, it's not the speed but the intensity of the speed. Most people lift weights quickly to make the lift easier—by allowing the momentum to lift the weight for them. What we're doing is using speed to make the lift more intense—big difference!

MINIMAL REDUNDANCY: Because most of us are fatigue seekers, many resistance-training programs and philosophies insist upon several exercises for each muscle group to "attack the muscle from every angle." Well, for starters, muscles need not be "attacked," but let's look at a typical chest workout that reflects old-school, follow-the-rules thinking.

First exercise: Bench press: 3 × 5 or 6

Second exercise: Incline dumbbell bench press: 3 × 8–10

Third exercise: Pec dec: 3 × 10–12

Fourth exercise: Cable crossover: 3 × 10–12

I'm sure you've seen guys doing a workout like this at the gym and wondered how on earth they could find the time or energy to train the rest of their bodies while using so many exercises per muscle group. Suffice it to say that a lot of guys train only chest and arms!

Now, it is true that some muscles—pectorals included—do have more than one attachment site and therefore might be more completely stimulated by more than one exercise. But in most cases, the benefit doesn't really outweigh the cost. In the above example, there is only a moderate difference in muscle activation between the first two exercises and only a minimal difference between the third and fourth exercises. If you trimmed that workout down to the first two exercises, you'd still get 98 percent of the benefit, with only half the time and effort. EDT is more efficient, because it focuses on the 80/20 principle, so to speak. If doing one pec exercise delivers 80 percent as much result as doing three pec exercises, it's more efficient to do the one exercise, especially for people who are short on time and energy.

LIFE BALANCE: The brevity of EDT workouts has a far-reaching benefit that escapes many trainees—you get to have a life. Most of us (incorrectly) assume that the best way to improve a particular skill or talent is to spend as much time and energy on it as possible. EDT is proof positive that this assumption isn't always true. You can achieve your fitness goals without sacrificing loads of time. You don't have to miss out on valuable time at work or with family to get the results you want. It's important to realize that your gym sessions will be most productive when you have a life to get back to once you're finished.

NEVER BEEN HERE BEFORE! PRS: YOUR OWN WORLD RECORDS

In the realm of sport, nothing compares to those rare moments when existing world records are broken. Only the rarest human beings can break world records, and even then, only rarely. Personally, I consider whether I could ever break a world record irrelevant—fortunately, it turns out! What really matters is this: Can you exceed your lifetime best performance? If you can, you're making progress and getting even closer to your ultimate destination.

In any given training session, there are several ways you can exceed your all-time best performance. You can increase the volume, intensity, and/or density of the workout while holding the exercise menu and session duration constant. You can also break your RM record for any given lift. Or you can meet or beat any of the above at a lighter body weight—an indicator of relative strength.

Unlike other training systems, Escalating Density Training is based upon a system of establishing and breaking PRs. This system allows you to regularly monitor and quantify your progress and then modify future workouts based on your performances. When your numbers are going up, you have proof that you're making progress, and emotional fuel to sustain your workouts.

A LOOK INSIDE THE PR ZONE

Although I constantly advise that the specific structure of EDT workouts should be natural and intuitive, I've nevertheless created a diagram of a hypothetical EDT session so that you can acquire a clearer appreciation of how EDT works.

EXERCISE	LOAD	REPS	APPROX. REST INTERVAL*
Set 1: Dips	175	5	12 sec
Set 2: Lat pulldowns	145	5	15 sec
Set 3: Dips	175	5	10 sec
Set 4: Lat pulldowns	145	5	14 sec
Set 5: Dips	175	5	13 sec
Set 6: Lat pulldowns	145	5	15 sec
Set 7: Dips	175	5	15 sec
Set 8: Lat pulldowns	145	5	17 sec
Set 9: Dips	175	5	15 sec
Set 10: Lat pulldowns	145	5	19 sec
Set 11: Dips	175	4	16 sec
Set 12: Lat pulldowns	145	4	21 sec
Set 13: Dips	175	4	24 sec
Set 14: Lat pulldowns	145	4	25 sec
Set 15: Dips	175	4	33 sec
Set 16: Lat pulldowns	145	4	34 sec
Set 17: Dips	175	3	42 sec
Set 18: Lat pulldowns	145	3	44 sec
Set 19: Dips	175	3	44 sec
Set 20: Lat pulldowns	145	3	47 sec
Set 21: Dips	175	2	51 sec
Set 22: Lat pulldowns	145	2	46 sec
Set 23: Dips	175	1	58 sec
Set 24: Lat pulldowns	145	1	102 sec

***Note:** *You're not seeking to achieve any specific rest intervals—this is simply to illustrate the typical rest-interval pattern that occurs during EDT workouts.*

Total elapsed time: 14 minutes, 51 seconds

Total sets per exercise: 12

Total sets for this PR Zone: 24

Total reps per exercise: 41 (i.e., your "PR")

Total reps for this PR Zone: 82

EDT LOADING PARAMETERS

In resistance training, whenever you're talking about sets and reps, rest periods, and so on, you're talking about loading parameters. Here are some principles to keep in mind.

■ EDT is based on the concept of doing progressively more work from workout to workout. Therefore, it's critical that your exercise biomechanics (a.k.a. technique) are consistent for every workout. If you perform strict curl form on one workout and lose that form on the next, you're not really doing more work.

■ Each EDT workout consists of between one and three PR Zones of 15-minute duration. Short rest periods of 5 minutes or so typically separate each PR Zone from the next.

■ During each PR Zone, you'll generally perform two exercises, for a total of three or four exercises per workout. Typically these exercises will be antagonistic and alternate back and forth, using the same weight for all sets, until the PR Zone has elapsed.

■ After warming up with the first exercise(s), you'll select a load that approximates a 10RM for each exercise. Ideally, the weight used for each exercise should be equally difficult.

■ Sets/reps/rest intervals: This is where EDT is truly unique. Most people will find it productive to do higher-repetition (but not maximal effort) sets with shorter rests at the beginning and then gradually progress to fewer reps per set and longer rest intervals as fatigue accumulates. For example, you might begin by performing sets of 5 with very short (10- to 15-second) rests. As you begin to fatigue, you'll increase your rest intervals as you drop down to sets of 4, then 2, and as the time limit approaches, you might crank out a few singles in an effort of accomplish as many repetitions as possible in the time allotted.

Note: Do not perform early sets to failure, or even near failure. My recommended starting point is to do half of what is possible (e.g., 5 reps with a 10RM weight) at the beginning of the time frame. As the time limit approaches, however, you should find yourself working at or near failure as you attempt to break your rep record.

■ Progression: Each time you repeat the workout, your objective is simply to perform more total repetitions in the same time frame. As soon as you can increase the total number of reps

Q&A

Q: *How many reps should I be completing in a 15-minute PR Zone? I feel like my weights might be too light.*

A: Ultimately, it won't really matter much, since EDT is a self-correcting system. If your weights are too light in any particular session, the system will direct you to add weight next time, and so on. Given that, here are some guidelines that will let you know that you're on track. My rule of thumb is that whenever you start a new exercise pairing, you should be getting approximately 50 repetitions per exercise per PR Zone. If you're off by 5 to 10 reps in either direction, don't worry about it. If, on the other hand, you're off by more than that, you may have chosen inadequate (if your numbers are too high) or excessive (if your numbers are too low) weights. Keep in mind, however, that as you repeat the same exercise pairing several times, your initial numbers will go down as your weights go up.

by 20 percent or more, begin the next workout with 5 percent more weight and start over. Similarly, if you manage to improve upon your last performance (for the same workout) by 40 percent, you'll increase your weights by 10 percent on the next workout. And so on.

YOU'VE ARRIVED AT YOUR DESTINATION! NOW WHAT?

Maybe the scariest aspect of goal orientation is the moment when you achieve your goal. What's the next step?

My suggestion is that you document your success. Use your training log or tracking software. This enables you to review your goal from inception to completion. It also fosters belief in your own abilities, especially as you accomplish more goals. Why do you think it's so universal that kindergarten kids receive stars or similar tokens as testament to their accomplishments? Why do you think Weight Watchers awards 10-, 20-, and 30-pound (and so on) ribbons to members when they lose the corresponding amount of weight? The answer is simple—to provide a visual reminder of the accomplishment. You should do the same, as silly as it may sound.

If your goal was designed to be a quantitative measure of a qualitative objective, did the fact that you accomplished the goal fulfill your objective? For example, if your objective was to increase the strength and size of your quads and hamstrings (qualitative) and you established a goal to increase your back squat by 50 pounds in 6 months (a quantitative goal), did the gain in your squat performance correlate with a significant gain in leg mass? If not, was accomplishing the goal worthwhile anyway, for other reasons? If the answer to either or both of the above is yes, you have solid results to base your future goal setting on.

Q&A

Q: *When I do a PR Zone, I usually find that I can keep doing sets of 5 the whole way through. Does this mean my weights are too light?*

A: Not necessarily. Remember that in EDT, the ends justify the means, and not the other way around. So as long as you can beat your PRs, it really doesn't matter if you do sets of 10 or sets of 2—just do whatever it takes to beat your PRs. I find, however, that over time most people will eventually gravitate to the more common pattern of starting with sets of 5, and then drop down to 4s, 3s and so on. You may be able to stay with sets of 5 for now, but assuming you're breaking your PRs, your weights are going to increase, and you'll probably get to the point where you'll need to drop your reps to continue breaking those PRs.

CHAPTER FIVE

PROGRAMMING FOR PERFORMANCE

WHEN I FIRST BEGAN PUBLISHING ARTICLES ON THE EDT SYSTEM, I heard from many people who raved about how it had made them stronger and faster. Some boasted of improved sprint times and vertical jumping ability. At first, these reports surprised me to some degree, because the programs I wrote about in those articles were designed as bodybuilding protocols, not strength-training or athletic-training programs. But after a bit of reflection, I developed a theory that explains why these individuals were experiencing such exciting gains in athletic performance. In short, I believe that many athletes today simply carry too much body fat. Fat is basically "nonfunctional" tissue—that is, it doesn't significantly contribute to strength, speed, power, agility, or almost any other athletic attribute you can think of. In fact, body fat is simply excess baggage that your muscles must carry around, which in turn decreases your performance potential.

In my own practice as a sports performance strategist, I've long noticed that you rarely see a particularly quick or agile athlete who carries more than 10 percent body fat. My colleague Martin Rooney, director of the Parisi Speed School in Fair Lawn, New Jersey, is one of the best

Q&A

Q: *I really like EDT but am more interested in strength than fat-loss bodybuilding. Can I just lower the reps, as long as I maintain the same principle (for example, start with sets of 3 with a 6RM weight)?*

A: Yes! By using a heavier weight, as you suggest, and preserving the fatigue-management technique of using half the possible number of reps per set, you'll create a powerful strength-development stimulus.

speed-development coaches in the country. When athletes come to Martin, trying to lower their 40-yard-dash times or to improve their vertical jumps, one of the first things he looks at is their body fat percentage. If it's more than 8 percent, Martin's staff will provide the athlete with a nutritional program to help decrease body fat level. My experiences mirror Martin's in this regard: Excess body fat diminishes your strength-to-weight ratio (also known as relative strength), which is critical to great athletic performance.

The bottom line is that EDT bodybuilding programs can quickly improve athletic performance simply by improving your body composition and strength-to-weight ratio. Once body fat levels are under 10 percent, however, you'll need to shift gears a bit if you want continued gains in athletic performance.

There are two primary characteristics you'll need to consider. The first is that your exercise selection should provide a high degree of dynamic correspondence, or specificity, to the skills you're trying to improve. One example of this concept would be the choice of barbell squats for a jumping athlete. Squats involve the same muscle groups as, and have a movement pattern similar to, that of vertical jumping. The similarity in movement pattern is most critical. Many athletes mistakenly choose, for example, leg presses, hack squats, or even Smith machine squats in an effort to improve their athletic abilities. While these exercise certainly do strengthen the involved muscle groups (and may make early contributions to performance by improving body composition), weight-training machines do not require the athlete to balance, stabilize, and control the resistance. The motor-control skills required for a leg press are completely dissimilar to those required for jumping. Not only does the leg press machine completely guide and control your movement, but you're also pushing the weight while lying on your back. Those interested in better athletic performance should choose free weights to gain balance, stability, and strength.

EDT PRINCIPLES FOR WEEKEND WARRIORS

Some people reading this book may be more interested in athletic performance than appearance, while others will find themselves locked into a "battle of goals"—that is, they want to perform better, but they also want a body that reflects their athleticism.

In truth, there is no need to feel conflicted if you seek both athletic performance and an aesthetically pleasing physique—these two goals are not contradictory in any way. Nevertheless, if performance is your primary objective, here are some key principles that you'll want to adhere to.

Principle One: **Unilateral or Bilateral?**

When considering what exercise choices to make, also remember that unilateral (single-limb) movements tend to transfer to many athletic skills better than bilateral exercises. After all, sprinting occurs one leg at a time, and so do most jumping skills. Punching, kicking, swinging, and striking are single-limb motor patterns as well. And beyond the specificity advantage, unilateral exercises tend to be safer for the spine. After all, you can't lunge with as much weight as you can squat, because you're using only one leg.

For these reasons, the sample program I've provided at the end of this chapter emphasizes unilateral movements over bilateral exercises, especially for lower-body movements.

Principle Two: **Prioritize Maximal Strength**

This critical principle for athletic enhancement is the prioritization of training methods that develop maximal strength. As noted earlier, there are many types of strength, and they all play a role in athletic performance. With that said, however, maximal strength—which is the amount of strength you can demonstrate in a single, all-out effort, such as performing a "1 rep max" in the weight room—deserves special emphasis, simply because it forms the foundation for every other strength quality. These include speed strength, the ability to move light or moderate loads very fast; strength speed, the ability to move heavy loads with great speed; and strength endurance, the ability to maintain strength in the face of fatigue.

Prioritizing maximal strength is a primary tenet of good "training economy," because you'll be able to accomplish several training objectives with one training method.

Principle Three: **Maximal Strength Development**

There are two primary methods athletes can use to develop the all-important strength quality of maximal strength. Both methods create high tensions in the muscle, which are the primary prerequisite for maximal strength development.

The first method involves using very heavy weights. This is the more familiar of the two methods, and it certainly produces results. Typical examples of training protocols using the "heavy-weight" method might include 6 sets of 2 repetitions using about 90 percent of 1RM (your single-repetition maximum, or 1 rep max) or 3 sets of 3 reps using about 85 percent of 1RM. Regardless of the percentages used, suffice it to say that this method normally involves using the heaviest possible weights for sets of between 1 and 3 repetitions.

While the heavy-weight method can certainly produce results, it's not without its drawbacks. Foremost among my concerns with this method is safety. The use of extremely heavy weights requires expert spotters, and even then, there is little room for error. When you're lifting the heaviest possible weight, you're moving very slowly—there's really a very small buffer zone between success and failure.

For this reason, I normally prefer an alternative method that produces equivalent results with a higher degree of safety. This method emphasizes the use of moderately heavy weights. By moderately heavy, I mean somewhere between 75 and 85 percent of 1RM for 2 or 3 reps per set, instead of very heavy or maximally heavy weights. Now, at any given speed, a heavier weight creates more muscular tension than a lighter weight. High muscular tensions are required for optimal maximal strength development. So to compensate for this, the weights are moved as fast as possible, particularly during the lifting portion of the rep. This method is called compensatory acceleration training (CAT)—a term coined by Fred Hatfield, PhD, back in the 1980s. Very simply, CAT means that you're compensating for the disadvantages posed by the lighter weight load by moving it faster.

This tactic creates the same tension magnitude as a heavier weight would, but it's safer, because when you start to fatigue, the worst thing that can happen is that you might not be quite as fast as you would like. With a maximally heavy weight, however, you have no buffer—that is, you're already moving very slowly since the weight is so heavy, so if you lose concentration or misjudge the effort required to lift the weight, you'll have to depend on your spotters for your safety. And unfortunately, spotters aren't always readily available.

Q&A

Q: *Sometimes I start a new PR Zone and quickly realize that the weights I'm using for both exercises aren't equally difficult. What do I do?*

A: I'd suggest "restarting" your workout. Just consider your earlier sets as an extended warmup. Most of the trial and error with EDT occurs the first time you perform a particular exercise pairing—after that, it's smooth sailing.

Q&A

Q: *How can I use EDT in a busy gym setting?*

A: I've created the programs in this book to work well in busy gym settings. Nevertheless, sometimes challenges crop up. One way to make sure that you'll never have a problem is to always use at least one barbell or dumbbell exercise in each PR Zone. That way, if the other exercise is on a machine or has to be performed at a fixed station, you can just carry the bar or dumbbells over to that station. If anyone asks how long you'll be using a particular station or piece of equipment, just tell them, "I'll be done in 8 minutes." It'll not only set them at ease; it'll show them you've got a plan!

Above and beyond the improved safety you'll experience using moderately heavy weights instead of maximally heavy weights, there's a psychological benefit as well. Extremely heavy weights can be daunting and, quite frankly, scary. And although many athletes are very good at ignoring or hiding their fears under heavy weights, the fact remains that these weights take their toll on your psyche. This toll extends the recovery time needed after a workout. With moderately heavy weights, it's a different story. It's actually fun and motivating to see how many reps you can complete. Certainly you know you won't need a life-or-death effort to lift the weight.

Principle Four: The Fatigue "Wake"

All workouts leave a fatigue "wake," meaning they produce fatigue, which will affect subsequent workouts to one degree or another. The effects of fatigue are specific. This means that, for example, the fatigue wake caused by a leg workout will have a more negative effect on a subsequent leg workout than it would have on a subsequent upper-body workout. Similarly, the fatigue wake from an aerobic workout will have a greater effect on a subsequent aerobic workout that it would have on an anaerobic workout.

Therefore, good planning involves a continual rotation of muscle groups, biomotor abilities, or both, in an effort to dissipate and reduce the possible negative effects of fatigue.

A SAMPLE ATHLETIC ENHANCEMENT TRAINING CYCLE

This training cycle utilizes an "A-B split." Basically, you'll train on three nonconsecutive days per week (Monday, Wednesday, and Friday, for instance), alternating between two different workouts (session 1 and session 2). Using this pattern, you'll perform both workouts six times over a 4-week training cycle. Here's an example of an A-B split.

FIRST PR ZONE (15 MINUTES)

A-1: DUMBBELL SNATCH (LEFT)

A-2: DUMBBELL SNATCH (RIGHT)

Begin by squatting low over a dumbbell. Maintain a locked and rigid lower back. Your feet should be about shoulder width apart. Grasp the dumbbell and tighten the abdominal muscles. In an explosive and continuous motion, accelerate the dumbbell upward until your arm is straight and locked. The dumbbell should travel close to the body and not swing out or away. Briefly hold it above the head, and then bring it down to the starting position. If necessary, you may assist the descent by using the opposite hand.

SECOND PR ZONE (15 MINUTES)

B-1: PULLUP

Pullups are performed with palms facing away from your body. Perform the pullup just like a lat pulldown, except that the body rises up to the bar, rather than the reverse. Keep the hips neutral, or parallel to the floor (knees may be flexed to avoid contact with the floor). Ensure that you clear the bar with your chin at the top, and allow your shoulder blades to spread apart at the bottom position. Think of pulling the elbows to the ribs, rather than lifting the chin over the bar. Chalk or lifting straps may be used to enhance the grip. Try to avoid flexing at the hips as fatigue accumulates. If needed, extra resistance may be provided through weight plates attached to a belt or by placing a dumbbell between the calves.

SECOND PR ZONE (15 MINUTES)

B-2: PUSH PRESS

Place a loaded bar on a rack at about your upper-chest level. Grasping the bar with both hands, lift it off the rack and support it on your shoulders. Dip the body by slightly bending the knees, hips, and ankles. Explosively drive upward with the legs, driving the barbell up off the shoulders and vigorously extending the arms overhead until your elbows are locked. Return to shoulders and repeat for the desired number of repetitions.

FIRST PR ZONE (15 MINUTES)

A-1: BULGARIAN SPLIT SQUAT (LEFT)

A-2: BULGARIAN SPLIT SQUAT (RIGHT)

Bulgarian split squats are essentially lunges performed one leg at a time (as opposed to alternating legs each rep) with the rear foot on top of a bench. Ensure that every rep (on both legs) is performed identically. This means that your left stance is exactly the same width and length as your right stance and that in the lunge position, your joint angles are always consistent. Also, make sure that your lead knee tracks directly over your lead foot (don't let your knee cave "inward") as you lunge.

Don't allow the curvature of your lower back to increase during the lunge. Although it's ideal to stand upright and erect as you lunge, it's okay to lean forward at the waist to keep your lumbar curvature neutral.

At the bottom of the split squat, your rear knee should be 3 to 4 inches away from the floor, and the front knee should be slightly ahead of your toes, with your torso completely upright and with a neutral lumbar spine.

If necessary, use dumbbells for additional resistance.

SECOND PR ZONE (15 MINUTES)

B-1: BENCH PRESS

Lie on the bench, placing both feet on the floor (if this causes the curvature of your lower back to increase, find a lower bench or place your feet on solid blocks to elevate them). Grasp the bar so that both hands are equidistant from the center, making sure your thumbs are wrapped around the bar, rather than on the same side as your other fingers. At the start, the bar should be directly over your nose—if it isn't, slide yourself up or down on the bench until it is. Inhale, and lift the bar from the supports. As you lower the bar to your chest, keep your elbows directly under it, rather than in front of or ahead of it. At the bottom of the movement, the bar should lightly touch your chest at nipple level. Return the bar to the starting position (it should actually travel up, as well as slightly back) by contracting your pectorals. *Always* employ a competent spotter when performing any bench press variation.

SECOND PR ZONE (15 MINUTES)

B-2: BENT BARBELL ROW

To perform this lift, a loaded bar should be positioned on the floor or on a low rack. Standing over the bar, lean down and grasp it with your palms facing your body. Lift the bar off the rack or floor, and stand, grasping the bar, both arms fully extended, very slightly bending at the knees, and bend at the hips so that the upper body is nearly parallel to the ground. Next, pull upward on the bar, flexing at the elbows and drawing the bar up to your lower chest at the bottom of the rib cage. This motion should be limited to the arms and upper back, and you should remain motionless at the legs and hips. Once the bar has been brought to the lower-chest area, lower the bar to the starting position, and repeat for the desired number of repetitions.

PART TWO

EDT PROGRAM MENUS

CHAPTER SIX

EDT PROGRAM DESIGN

NOW THAT WE'VE BUILT A FOUNDATION OF KNOWLEDGE BY REVIEWING the pitfalls of "traditional" weight training, and describing the essential principles of Escalating Density Training, it's time to further clarify our plan by presenting a menu of three different weekly training "splits." Unlike the authors of many books on the subject, I've decided against the common practice of categorizing these programs according to the reader's experience level (beginner, intermediate, and advanced, for example). This is because I want to dispel the common misconception that advanced trainees need to devote more time to their training than beginners do.

In my own experience, advanced athletes often need less time for two reasons. First, the longer you've been training, the smarter you'll get when it comes to efficiency in your workout. By this, I mean you'll eventually figure out what works, what doesn't, and how to get the most bang for your buck in the gym. You'll know when to focus on correcting weak areas of preparation and what time-consuming habits you can kick to save time. Second, competitive athletes and experienced recreational exercisers tend to overdo it—after all, part of their success is owed to the fact that they love to train. These individuals often experience renewed progress by cutting back on their overall training volume. Therefore, the programs in this book are organized around varying levels of time commitment.

Okay, it's time to create an effective weekly training split, including exercise selection, selection of loading strategies, and determining optional set/rep protocols. This is where we get into questions like:

- How should I set up my weekly split?
- What exercises should I use?
- How many exercises should I do?
- How often should I train?

Right at the outset, let me remind you about a few points made earlier. Remember to keep in mind that (1) there is no best way, (2) everything works, and (3) nothing works forever. Whenever you find yourself struggling with whether or not you've put together the "perfect" training cycle or chosen the "right" number of exercises, you can relax. There is no best solution to any of these questions, and even if there were, after a handful of weeks your body would become accustomed to whatever you've put together, and you'd have to write up a new program anyway.

With that in mind, I'd like to share a very simple and effective way of conceptualizing the process of program design.

STEP ONE:
DETERMINE WHICH MUSCLE YOU WANT/NEED TO TRAIN

Many people will choose to train every major muscle group, but some people, because of injuries, equipment restrictions, or other factors, may do better by omitting one or more major muscle groups. For the purposes of this discussion, however, I'll assume that you'll be training your whole body. Your list will look something like this.

- Quadriceps
- Hamstrings
- Hip flexors
- Calf muscles (gastrocnemius and soleus)
- Leg adductors
- Leg abductors
- Abdominals (rectus abdominis, obliques, and transverse abdominis)
- Chest (pectoralis major and minor)

- Upper back (latissimus dorsi, teres major and minor, rhomboids, trapezius)
- Lower back
- Glutes
- Deltoids (three heads)

IS ISOLATION NECESSARY?

Not only is isolation not necessary, it's not even possible! The brain's motor cortex will normally select a movement pattern that allows more muscle groups to participate in the effort, in order to conserve energy and avoid dangerous levels of stress to any single muscle involved in the movement. So multijoint movement patterns are not just a matter of efficiency; they're also an important safety mechanism. Soft-tissue therapist Deane Juhan offers the following observation in his book *Job's Body*:

> ***Let us imagine ourselves observing a person who is standing erect and executing the simple gesture of raising their straight right arm to the side until it is horizontal. The fibers in the deltoid, the supraspinatus, and the upper trapezius will contract to produce the primary motion, while the fibers of the pectoral major, the pectoral minor, and latissimus dorsi must simultaneously extend to allow it. But the contraction of the right trapezius will not only raise the right arm, it will also tend to pull the neck toward the right; therefore, the left trapezius, along with the other muscles of the neck, will have to contract as well in order to stabilize it. Furthermore, the extended right arm will overbalance the torso to the right, so the erector spinae muscles on the left side of the spine must contract to brace the whole torso and keep it erect. And since this contraction of the left erector spinae set will tend to pull the left side of the pelvis up as well, the gluteus medius and minimus of the left side must also brace to hold the pelvis level. Since not only the torso, but the body as a whole is threatened with tipping by the overbalancing weight of the extended arm, the right leg must brace as well, using fibers in the hip, the thigh, the calf, the feet, the toes.***

While there are exceptions to every rule, for the most part selecting exercises that require multiple muscles to function simultaneously tends to be a safer, more efficient, and more functional way to train.

■ Biceps

■ Triceps

STEP TWO:
ASSIGN EACH MUSCLE TO A DAY OF THE WEEK

Again, there is no single best way but, rather, many possible ways to do this. Here are a few examples to get you started.

Sample Training Split #1

In this split, you're lifting 4 days a week. Larger muscle groups generally need longer recovery periods than smaller muscles, and that's why quads, hamstrings, pecs, and lats are trained only once a week, whereas biceps and triceps are trained twice—directly on Thursdays and indirectly on Mondays.

Monday: Pecs, lats, shoulders

Tuesday: Quads and hamstrings

Wednesday: Off

Thursday: Biceps and triceps

Friday: Off

Saturday: Calves and abs

Sunday: Off

Sample Training Split #2

This is an example of a "3-day split" with a structure similar to the first split we looked at. The primary difference is that this split contains no direct work for abs or calves. This arrangement may or may not be warranted for your particular situation, but as an example, if your abs and calves are already strong and well developed (perhaps from martial arts participation, genetics, or other factors), it's likely to work quite well.

Monday: Quads and hamstrings

Tuesday: Off

Wednesday: Biceps and triceps

Thursday: Off

Friday: Pecs, lats, shoulders

Saturday: Off

Sunday: Off

Sample Training Split #3

Here we have a 4-day split in which pecs are trained with biceps on one day, and lats with triceps on another day. The rationale? Most pec exercises heavily involve the triceps, and the antagonists of the triceps are your biceps. Similarly, most lat exercises make strong use of the biceps, which are antagonistic to the triceps.

Monday: Quads, hamstrings, and abs

Tuesday: Off

Wednesday: Pecs and biceps

Thursday: Off

Friday: Lats and triceps

Saturday: Shoulders

Sunday: Off

Sample Training Split #4

"Whole-body training" refers to the use of large, multijoint exercises, such as squats, bench presses, deadlifts, chins, and dips. These exercises challenge large muscular regions and for the most part eliminate the need for direct exercises for the smaller muscle groups. This method is ideal for athletes and others whose time and energy are at a premium.

Monday: Whole body

Tuesday: Off

Wednesday: Whole body

Thursday: Off

Friday: Whole body

Saturday: Off

Sunday: Off

The A-B Split

The programs presented in this book use a lesser-known but tremendously effective body-part split known as the A-B split. This is a super-simple way to organize your training, and over the years, I've used it with great success with hundreds of clients. Quite simply, you create two workouts—a session 1 and a session 2. Next, you divide your list of muscles into two groups, assigning half of them to session and half to session 2. There are many ways this can be done—here is one example, where upper-body muscles are assigned to session 1 and lower-body muscles are assigned to session 2.

CONSIDER THE ADVANTAGES OF SETTING UP A HOME GYM

While health club memberships have their advantages and work well for some people, for others a home gym is a better option. Better yet: Why not install a simple home gym even if you have a health club membership? This way, you've got more options and fewer excuses.

The home gym offers lots of advantages that a commercial gym can't. For starters, it's always there and it's never crowded. You won't need to pack your gym bag, find the car keys, fight traffic, find a parking spot, or wait in line for the equipment you want to use. In fact, you don't even need to change into your gym clothes. These advantages add up to some pretty significant savings in time, stress, and energy expenditure, not to mention the money you'll save by canceling your gym membership.

Many people assume they don't have enough money or space for a home gym, but most people do in fact have the resources necessary to convert a small area of their home or apartment into a workout area. Often, one side of the garage or basement will make an ideal training area. Here are my suggestions for an inexpensive and maximally efficient training area at home.

1. A squat cage with attached chinning bar. This is the centerpiece of your training area. Most cages are about 7 feet tall and require about 35 square feet of floor space. You can buy one new from any of the companies I've listed in the Resources section on page 223, or you can hunt for one in your local classifieds. It's not hard to find a secondhand cage (or power rack, as they're sometimes called) for $100 or so. Try to find a rack with plate-storage pegs integrated into the unit—this will save you from having to buy plate trees and save you money and floor space. A squat cage will permit the performance of dozens of key exercises, including squats, bench presses, overhead presses, chins and

SESSION 1	SESSION 2
Pecs	Quads
Lats	Hamstrings
Shoulders	Glutes
Biceps	Gastrocnemius
Triceps	Soleus
Forearms	Abs

pullups, and curls, just to name a few.

2. An adjustable bench. Again, check the recommended companies in the Resources section, or check the classifieds. A bench is essential for all forms of bench pressing as well as many other exercises. When it's not in use, store the bench inside the rack to save space.

3. A 300-pound Olympic barbell set. This can be bought new for $100 or less—and often much cheaper secondhand. Needless to say, a barbell set is indispensable. As with your bench, the bar will normally sit inside your rack.

4. A set of Power Block selectorized dumbbells. Power Blocks are one of the greatest inventions the gym industry has seen in the past 50 years. Basically, they are an entire dumbbell set that occupies the same space as a single pair of dumbbells. Different weight options are available, and I recommend also buying the stand. See the Resources section for more information.

Once these essentials are in place, you're obviously free to augment your home gym with other items as the need and opportunity arise. Nevertheless, I could effectively train the highest-caliber Olympic athlete with the four items listed above, so don't fall into the trap of thinking that you need all sorts of specialized equipment to be successful, because you don't. Despite "advances" in equipment technology, no one has ever been able to improve upon the low-tech standards—barbells and dumbbells. Some of the strongest and most muscular men who've ever lived trained with these tools—and without modern advances in nutrition and supplementation. If you haven't considered home training before reading this, I strongly urge you to do so. EDT is ideal for home gym applications, and I consider training at home to be an essential strategy for maximum results if you're crunched for time.

Note: I've assigned abdominals to session 2—that's because many leg exercises, such as squats, heavily involve the abs anyway.

You can also mix things up and assign both upper- and lower-body muscles to each session. Here's an example of that approach.

SESSION 1	SESSION 2
Pecs	Lats
Quads	Hamstrings
Shoulders	Glutes
Gastrocnemius	Biceps
Triceps	Soleus
Abs	Forearms

Be Creative!

There is no absolute right or wrong way to put training splits together—many possibilities exist. Don't be afraid to be creative, even if it means you might make a few mistakes along the way—we all do, and it's a necessary part of the learning process.

STEP THREE: ASSIGN EXERCISES FOR EACH MUSCLE GROUP

Once you've constructed a split, designate exercises for each muscle group. This does require some specific knowledge, but most readers, especially if they've been training awhile, will already have a pretty good sense of how to do this.

While it's not a bad idea to challenge your muscles with various exercises, you won't need to do so in the space of a single workout. Instead, you can train each major muscle group every 3 or 4 days and use different exercises each time. For example, we can split a chest and biceps workout in two, like this:

Q&A

Q: *Can I substitute different exercises with the programs in this book?*

A: Absolutely. The programs I present in this book are provided as specific examples so you can better understand how the EDT system works. By all means, I encourage creativity!

MONDAY

A. Bench press

B. Barbell curl

C. 45-degree-incline dumbbell curl

THURSDAY

A. 45-degree-incline dumbbell bench press

B. Concentration curl

C. Pec dec

With this arrangement, you'll get the best of both worlds—each muscle will get a variety of challenges across two workouts, and at the same time, you'll have a lot more time and energy to devote to each muscle during each workout.

MASTERING THE WARMUP

The great observational comedian George Carlin once quipped, "No one jumps out of bed and starts vacuuming, do they?" Unfortunately, the way that most people warm up is the equivalent of doing just that!

Warming up is a skill that belongs in your toolbox of basics. And while many people are constantly on the lookout for new or unique ways to achieve success in the gym, *truly* successful people are those who've learned to appreciate and master basic skills.

A perfect warmup virtually ensures a perfect workout, but a poor one will almost certainly ruin what *could* have been a great training experience. Ever wake up dreading the idea of going to the gym but, after getting there, end up having a great workout? You can thank your warmup for that. Think of a warmup as a transition from a low level of activity to a high level of activity.

As with most training-related subjects, there are various approaches to warming up that can and do work. This is my approach, and it's yielded great results for hundreds of clients over the years. If you've never paid particular attention to your warmup routine, let me remind you that once addressed, the elements you tend to ignore usually have the most potential for improving your overall rate of progress!

DOES WARMING UP WORK?

Both research and anecdotal evidence on the benefits of warming up is extensive and almost universally supportive, so I won't spend a lot of time elaborating on the merits of the warmup procedure—I think we all understand the importance, even if only on a gut level.

Let me just briefly say that it is well known that warming up increases central nervous system function (improving such qualities as coordination and reaction speed, to name two), makes muscles more pliable, and facilitates joint lubrication. A proper warmup also reduces the perception of effort when performing difficult physical tasks such as weight training.

I would like to add another potential benefit that is rarely addressed: The warmup allows you to assess your health status and make corrections before you hurt yourself. If, for example, you have chronic, off-and-on problems with a particular muscle or joint (where sometimes you can train with it or around it and other times you can't), you can monitor your status as the warmup proceeds and, if necessary, make an exercise substitution before the workout commences. The longer you've trained, the more you'll appreciate the importance of this.

The basic idea of a good warmup is to prepare yourself adequately for the intense work to come, without fatiguing yourself in the process. From my observations, however, many people either perform too little work or do so much that their warmups become workouts. With practice and experience, you'll learn to find the "sweet spot" that leads to optimal performance.

THE THREE-STAGE WARMUP

I view the perfect EDT warmup as a three-stage process.

Stage 1: The Mental Warmup

Experienced trainees tend to think all week about the impending workout. They rehearse the workout dozens of times in their minds and are aware of the problems they might encounter (such as rush hour in the gym or a nagging hamstring pull that might kick up during the workout). A novice trainee, on the other hand, doesn't know what he will do until he gets to the gym (and maybe not even then!). Since novices typically get novice-level results, I urge you to explore visualization and autogenic training, which are established methods of maximizing physical performance in training and in competition. Some people learn these techniques on their own, while others need instruction. Either way, *use* them!

Stage 2: Elevate Core Temperature (the General Warmup)

Begin the physical warmup sequence with low-intensity cardiovascular activity for 3 to 5 minutes, or until you break a sweat. Although almost anything will do, my preferred mode of activity for this stage of the warmup is skipping rope, for several reasons.

- A jump rope is inexpensive and portable—it can be done anywhere.
- Skipping rope gives my clients the opportunity to develop reactive strength in the lower limbs, which creates a good foundation for jumping and plyometric drills.
- As I watch my client skip rope, I can get a rough idea of his or her nervous system

status by the level of timing and coordination that he or she displays during the skipping session. If my athlete is tripping all over herself, then we need a more extensive warmup than what might have been originally planned.

I'm often asked if it's okay to skip this section of the warmup when you're tight on time or if you simply find warming up to be a bother. And the answer is that yes, the warmup can be skipped, but more times than not, you'll have a better workout when you complete one, because you'll achieve a better physical and psychological transition between inactivity and an intense workout.

Stage 3: Skill Rehearsal and Load Selection (the Specific Warmup)

Once your general warmup has been completed, it's time to determine your "working" weights (this applies only to the first time you do a new PR Zone, of course—if you're repeating a PR Zone that you've already performed, you'll already know your starting weights).

Let's assume your first PR Zone for the workout involves hack squats and lat pulldowns. Your goal is to identify how much weight to use for each exercise. That weight should be your 10RM (a weight you can lift 10 times before reaching absolute muscular failure) for each movement, but it's okay if you're off by a rep or two. More important, as you perform your warmup sets, you're trying to make sure that the weights you select for each exercise are equally difficult. Here's a hypothetical scenario that illustrates how that process might work.

You load a couple of 45-pound plates on the hack squat machine, take your position, unhook the safety mechanism, and perform 5 reps, making a mental note of how difficult it felt. Next, you walk over to the lat pulldown station and place the pin at the 60-pound level. You position yourself under the thigh pads, grab the bar, and perform 5 reps. You notice that this was a bit easier than your set of 5 on the hack squat machine. You add 50 pounds on the hack squat and perform another 5 reps and notice that this feels like it might be your 10RM. Back to the lat pulldowns—you increase the weight to 100 pounds, and after about 3 reps, you realize you've gone a bit too heavy. So you stop after the 4th rep and decide to use 90 pounds as your working weight for pulldowns.

With your weights established, you're ready to start your 15-minute PR Zone. The specific warmup just described took only about 5 minutes, but in some situations the specific warmup might take upwards of 10 minutes. Generally speaking, older people training in the morning in colder climates will require a slightly longer warmup, whereas younger trainees working out later in the day in warmer climates won't need as much time to warm up.

And just to reiterate: If you've already performed a particular PR Zone, you'll already know your working weights every time you repeat it. This tends to reduce the time necessary to warm up for it. In these cases, my suggestion is to perform each exercise for 2 or 3 sets of 3 reps, using your prescribed working weight on each set. Then you're ready to start the timer and get to work.

WHAT ABOUT COOLDOWNS?

Although some training experts recommend a formal cooldown (which typically resembles the general warmup discussed earlier), I don't think the benefits outweigh the costs. More important than a physical cooldown is a mental cooling-off period. Maybe listen to some relaxing music while you finish making your training log entries, or do some light stretching while your body is nice and warm. These activities help you transition to a lower level of physical activity and allow you to savor the "endorphin rush" created by the workout.

A FEW FINAL THOUGHTS AND RECOMMENDATIONS

Before we move on to the various program examples, I'd like to share some observations about effective program design. Keep these rules of thumb in mind when you're putting your own programs together or thinking about following a program from a book or magazine. While these are not absolute rules, often you'll be better off following them.

1. Any program intense enough to create results is also intense enough to cause overtraining—eventually. I recommend taking 1 week completely off after every 8 weeks of weight training.

2. Most people get the best results from training 3 or 4 days a week. Training more frequently than this will almost always lead to problems.

3. All workouts should be completed in 60 minutes or less, and 45 minutes is even better.

4. Whenever possible, choose compound (multijoint) exercises over isolation exercises. Generally, the more muscles hit by a single exercise, the more effective it is.

5. Whenever possible, choose free weights over machines. Free weights force you to control the weights you're lifting, which leads to greater muscle growth.

6. If a muscle you're planning to train today is still sore from a previous workout, wait until the soreness has disappeared.

Don't be rigid with your programs. If something's hurting, or if you're sore or dreading the workout, don't be afraid to make a change on the fly. Training should be fun, at least most of the time.

CHAPTER SEVEN

45 MINUTES PER WEEK

ANYONE WITH A FEW YEARS OF GYM TIME UNDER THEIR BELTS WILL assume that 45 minutes a week in the gym is simply not enough time to see noteworthy results. While this may be true for some people, I nevertheless recommend that those with no prior experience with EDT—regardless of how much time they've spent with other methods of training—use this 45-minute program for 3 or 4 weeks before moving up to the more advanced programs in Chapters Eight and Nine.

These are 3-day-per-week programs, and each program (along with the other programs in this section) employs an A-B split, which simply means that you'll alternate between two different workouts. Assuming you train on Mondays, Wednesdays, and Fridays, your schedule will look like this.

WEEK 1

Monday: Perform session 1

Wednesday: Perform session 2

Friday: Perform session 1

WEEK 2

Monday: Perform session 2

Wednesday: Perform session 1

Friday: Perform session 2

WHAT IS GOOD FORM?

I define "good form" a bit differently than most. Good form to me means maintaining pain-free optimal body alignment and range of motion on every repetition.

GENERAL FORM GUIDELINES FOR ALL WEIGHT-TRAINING EXERCISES

The following recommendations should be monitored for all weight-training exercises. It's important to be *proactive* when it comes to exercise technique. Don't just assume that you're doing it correctly—actively *look* for possible errors until your technique has become optimized and stable. Mirrors, video recording, and qualified training partners and coaches are all great forms of feedback.

Pain is to be avoided, not sought. We're all different, with unique postural and orthopedic histories. If you're doing a particular exercise and it causes pain, *stop.* Even if you've got the best coaches looking at you, and every weight-training book ever written says that your form is perfect, it isn't. Pain means that whatever you're doing is causing harm to your body. Remember that some people cannot safely perform particular movement patterns, because of injuries or other factors. I, for example, cannot perform a "perfect" deep squat (even though I understand how to perform one), because I've had serious knee surgeries that have left me with range-of-motion restrictions caused by scar tissue buildup. I've learned to modify my squats (primarily by reducing the range of motion) in such a way that I can perform them safely. If an exercise causes pain, discontinue that exercise and seek competent instruction (see the Resources section in this book to find qualified instruction in your area). If the pain persists, seek qualified medical attention to determine the cause of the pain.

Always lift with the whole body. During any exercise, keep the noninvolved muscles tight and *bolted down*—which means that even during so-called isolation exercises, such as barbell curls, every muscle in your body should be participating through static or isometric contraction. It's truly the *opposite* of isolation. Russian kettlebell expert Pavel Tsatsouline suggested the following experiment while teaching at one of my annual boot camps. Reach out and shake your partner's hand as tightly as possible (make sure he can handle it first!); then disengage. Next, tighten up your abs and glutes as hard as you can, and repeat the handshake. Your partner will notice that your grip strength has suddenly skyrocketed! The tension created in your abs and glutes serves to increase tension in all your other muscles as well. This is called "hyperirradiation."

Consistent performance is key. Every rep should look *exactly* the same, except for speed. It's okay to slow down during a set—as fatigue accumulates, that'll be a given. It's *not* okay if your 1st rep looks like a squat and your 10th rep looks like a curtsy! Envision yourself as a machine: The 1st rep looks just like every other rep, with no variation at all, other than the inevitable slowing down as fatigue sets in.

Ensure and maintain left-right symmetry. During bilateral (two-limb) exercises—such as barbell curls, squats, seated rows, bench presses, and deadlifts—the left and right sides of your body should be doing *exactly* the same thing, with no variance in range of motion or posture. Use a video camera, or get a training partner, to see if, for instance, one hip rises more than the other on squats. Or maybe on bench presses your right elbow flares out more than the left. Hone your awareness by watching others at the gym—this is the fastest way to learn, aside from hiring a skilled coach.

When using weight-training machines, ensure that the working joint is lined up with the machine's axis of rotation. For example, during leg extensions, the pad or roller that you push against with your shins shouldn't slide or move up and down your shin as you lift the weight. If it does, adjust your seat position until you solve the problem.

(15-MINUTE PR ZONE AFTER WARMUPS)

A-1: HACK SQUAT

Position yourself under the hack squat machine's shoulder supports and place your feet symmetrically on the foot platform. Keep in mind that a higher foot placement intensifies the training stress on the glute and hamstring muscles (especially if you push from the heels), while a relatively lower foot placement tends to throw the brunt of the load onto your quadriceps (especially if you push from your forefoot).

Once you've established your position on the machine, disengage the safety mechanism and descend into a semisquat by flexing at your hips and knees. Complete the rep by returning to the starting position. Make sure to reengage the safety mechanism before exiting the machine.

(15-MINUTE PR ZONE AFTER WARMUPS)

A-2: LAT PULLDOWN

Grasp the bar with your hands slightly wider than shoulder width apart with palms facing away from your body. Next, pull the bar down toward your clavicle by contracting the latissimus dorsi ("lats") and elbow flexor muscles. Return to the starting position.

LOCKING OUT YOUR JOINTS

The notion that one shouldn't lock out joints during weight-training exercises probably got started in the bodybuilding community, where fatigue seeking was developed into a fine art decades ago. The rationale works like this: Let's say you're doing a set of leg presses. At the end of the lifting stage of each rep, it's possible to lock out your knees and take almost all the tension off your working muscles. If you're a fatigue seeker, this is bad—training is supposed to hurt, after all! If you're a performance seeker, however, "rest-pausing" between reps is actually a great way of improving performance by managing (as opposed to seeking) pain and fatigue. Once again: Seek performance by managing pain, not seeking pain!

Many people will protest that locking out joints is dangerous and will lead to injury. Nothing could be further from the truth, however while you should *allow* your joints to fully straighten when you complete a rep, you shouldn't slam your joints into full extension. Doing so can eventually lead to contracture—a condition where the shortened muscle will no longer allow your joints to fully straighten.

(15-MINUTE PR ZONE AFTER WARMUPS)

A-1: CHEST PRESS MACHINE

Position yourself on the seat of the chest press machine. Although some machines vary, for the most part you'll want to adjust the seat (up or down) so that your shoulders start off directly in front of the handles. It's also a good idea to check each machine's instruction card for proper positioning tips. Once your seat position is established, simply grasp the handles and push the mechanism straight away from you. Complete the rep by reversing this motion.

FORM RECOMMENDATIONS FOR UPPER-BODY LIFTING

- **Ensure an even, balanced grip or hand placement. On barbell exercises, for example, be certain that your hands are equidistant from the center of the bar, and *always* keep your thumbs wrapped around the bar.**
- **Keep your lower body rigid and locked down.**
- **Keep eyes on the horizon (during standing lifts) or straight ahead (on seated or lying lifts). *Never* turn your head during *any* weight-training exercise.**
- **Avoid upper-body flexion. This is common during heavy barbell curls, for example: As the going gets tough, there's a tendency to hunch forward and drop the chin to the chest. This is an attempt by your nervous system to recruit more strength for the job, but it's not a safe strategy, so be aware of this tendency and adjust your weights accordingly to avoid it. During standing exercises, a common cue is "Big chest" or "Chest up!"**

(15-MINUTE PR ZONE AFTER WARMUPS)

A-2: BACK EXTENSION

Perform this exercise by positioning yourself on a back extension machine. Adjust your position so that your hips are slightly forward of the support pad, which ensures that your pelvis can rotate during the exercise. Starting with the hips flexed at a 90-degree angle, raise yourself to a horizontal position by contracting the spinal erectors (lower-back muscles), glutes, and hamstrings. Pause, and then lower yourself to the starting position.

FIRST PR ZONE (15 MINUTES)

A-1: BULGARIAN SPLIT SQUAT (LEFT)

A-2: BULGARIAN SPLIT SQUAT (RIGHT)

With your back foot resting on a bench, lower your body until the knee of your rear leg almost touches the floor. Pause; then raise yourself until your front knee is nearly straight. Maintain an upright torso throughout.

FIRST PR ZONE (15 MINUTES)

A-1: DUMBBELL THRUSTER

Assume a standing position with a dumbbell in each hand. Your arms should be in front of your torso, simulating a boxer's guard position. Descend into a squat position. At the deepest point, the tops of your thighs should be parallel to the floor when viewed from the side. Immediately ascend, and as you reach a standing position, immediately and seamlessly press the dumbbells overhead with arms locked. Lower the dumbbells back to your shoulders.

Note: There should not be a pause between the completion of the squat and the initiation of the dumbbell press—it should be a single continuous motion. Maintain an upright posture and neutral spine throughout. Do not pause between reps.

FIRST PR ZONE (15 MINUTES)

A-2: PULLUP (ON CHIN/DIP ASSIST UNIT)

Grasp a chinning bar with an overhand grip approximately shoulder width apart. From a hanging position, pull yourself up until your chin clears the bar. Reverse this motion to return to the starting position. Avoid flexing from the hips when performing pullups or chins.

FIRST PR ZONE (15 MINUTES)

A-1: DEADLIFT

Assume a standing position immediately behind a loaded barbell. Adjust your feet so that they point straight ahead or are slightly angled out. Maintain a neutral spine at all times (that is, don't allow your lower back to round). Keep your weight toward your heels as you crouch down to grasp the bar with an overhand grip. From this position, simply stand up through an active extension of your hips and knees.

Ensure that the bar stays in close contact with the front of your shins throughout. Use a deliberate tempo with minimal momentum. When viewed from the side, your hips and shoulders should ascend together; if the hips rise before the shoulders, it means you're using your back rather than your legs.

FIRST PR ZONE (15 MINUTES)

A-2: BENCH PRESS

Lie faceup on the bench, placing both feet on the floor. Grasp the bar such that both hands are equidistant from the center, and make sure your thumbs are wrapped around the bar, rather than on the same side as your other fingers. At the start, the bar should be directly over your nose—if it isn't, slide yourself up or down on the bench until it is. Inhale and unrack the bar from the supports. As you lower the bar to your chest, keep your elbows directly under the bar, rather than in front of or ahead of the bar. At the bottom of the movement, the bar should lightly touch your chest at nipple level. Return the bar to the starting position (it should actually travel up, as well as slightly back) by contracting your pectorals.

***Always* employ a competent spotter when performing any bench press variation.**

FIRST PR ZONE (15 MINUTES)

A-1: MILITARY PRESS

Place a loaded bar on a rack at about your upper-chest level. Grasping the bar with both hands, lift it off the rack and support it on your shoulders. From this position, drive the barbell up off the shoulders, vigorously extending arms overhead until your elbows are locked. Keep your back and legs locked throughout. Reverse this motion to complete the rep.

FIRST PR ZONE (15 MINUTES)

A-2: STIFF-LEG DEADLIFT

Set up a barbell at slightly higher than knee level (use a power rack, or set the barbell on blocks). Using an overhand grip, grab the bar with a shoulder-width grip, and step back just enough to clear the rack. Inhale, slightly bend the knees, and begin the movement while maintaining your body weight over your heels. Allow the bar to descend while you ensure it maintains contact with the front of your body. While descending, maintain the normal curvature of the lower back and neck, and allow the glutes to move rearward. Do not look up, but instead maintain a normal head and neck alignment. Always use a controlled-movement speed with this exercise. Never perform it rapidly or explosively.

FIRST PR ZONE (15 MINUTES)

A-1: BACK SQUAT

Position the barbell on the support pins inside of a power rack such that the bar is level with your mid-chest. Place safety pins on each side at a position slightly lower than your intended deepest position. Place your hands evenly on the bar (a close grip with elbows under the bar will allow for a more upright posture), and with your feet squarely under the bar, lift it from the rack by extending your legs.

Step back enough to avoid bumping the rack during the exercise, and position your feet shoulder width apart. The weight should remain centered over the back half of the feet, not on the heels or toes. Slowly descend into a near-bottom position, keeping the torso and back erect so that the hips remain under the bar. Do not allow the hips to drift backward or the torso to incline forward.

When viewed from the side, the angles formed at the knee joint and hip joint should be close to equal. Also, your hips and shoulders should ascend together—if the hips rise before the shoulders, it means you're using your back rather than your legs. Rise out of the squat position following the same path that you descended—your torso and back erect, and your hips under the bar throughout the ascent.

A-2: CHINS (ON CHIN/DIP ASSIST UNIT)

Grasp a chinning bar with an underhand grip approximately shoulder width apart. From a hanging position, pull yourself up until your chin clears the bar. Reverse this motion to return to the starting position. Avoid flexing from the hips when performing pullups or chins.

This exercise is performed the same way as pullups, except that chins are performed with your palms facing toward you, which increases biceps involvement. The closer the grip, the more the biceps are involved. Chalk or lifting straps may be used to secure a good grip.

FIRST PR ZONE (15 MINUTES)

A-1: PUSH PRESS

Place a loaded bar on a rack at about your upper-chest level. Grasping the bar with both hands, lift it off the rack and support it on your shoulders. Dip the body by bending the knees, hips, and ankles slightly. Explosively drive upward with the legs, driving the barbell up off the shoulders, vigorously extending arms overhead until your elbows are locked. Reverse this motion to complete the rep.

FIRST PR ZONE (15 MINUTES)

A-2: BACK EXTENSION

Perform this exercise by positioning yourself on a back extension machine. Adjust your position so that your hips are slightly forward of the support pad, which ensures that your pelvis can rotate during the exercise. Starting with the hips flexed at a 90-degree angle, raise yourself up to a horizontal position by contracting the spinal erectors, glutes, and hamstrings. Pause, and lower yourself to the starting position.

FIRST PR ZONE (15 MINUTES)

A-1: PISTOL (RIGHT)

A-2: PISTOL (LEFT)

Directions for right side: **Stand in front of a bench, and extend both arms straight in front of you. Next, extend your left foot and leg so that your heel is just off the floor at all times. From this position, lower yourself to the bench under complete control by bending your right knee and keeping your support foot flat on the floor. Pause briefly and return to the starting position. Finish the reps on the right side, and then repeat the same motion for the reps on the left side.**

FIRST PR ZONE (15 MINUTES)

A-1: BENCH PRESS

Lie faceup on the bench, placing both feet on the floor. Grasp the bar such that both hands are equidistant from the center, and make sure your thumbs are wrapped around the bar, rather than on the same side as your other fingers. At the start, the bar should be directly over your nose—if it isn't, slide yourself up or down on the bench until it is. Inhale, and unrack the bar from the supports. As you lower the bar to your chest, keep your elbows directly under the bar, rather than in front of or ahead of the bar. At the bottom of the movement, the bar should lightly touch your chest at nipple level. Return the bar to the starting position (it should actually travel up, as well as slightly back) by contracting your pectorals.

***Always* employ a competent spotter when performing any bench press variation.**

FIRST PR ZONE (15 MINUTES)

A-2: LOW CABLE ROW

Attach a straight bar to the low cable mechanism. Next, take a seated position with your feet on the bracing plates. Keeping both knees slightly bent, take an overhand grip on the bar and pull the handle to your lower abdomen. Reverse this motion to complete the rep. Maintain a fixed torso throughout, and be sure to actively squeeze your shoulder blades together at the completion of the pull.

FIRST PR ZONE (15 MINUTES)

A-1: DUMBBELL SNATCH (LEFT)

A-2: DUMBBELL SNATCH (RIGHT)

Begin by squatting low over a dumbbell. Maintain a locked and rigid lower back. The feet should be about shoulder width apart. Grasp the dumbbell and tighten the abdominal muscles. In an explosive and continuous motion, accelerate the dumbbell upward until your arm is straight and locked. The dumbbell should travel close to the body and not swing out or away. Briefly hold it above the head and then bring it down to the starting position. If necessary, you may assist the descent by using the opposite hand.

FIRST PR ZONE (15 MINUTES)

A-1: DIPS (ON CHIN/DIP ASSIST UNIT)

Descend slowly and under complete control. Maintain a vertical torso for more shoulder and triceps involvement, and a forward lean to increase pectoral recruitment. Be careful not to exceed your shoulder's range of motion. Return back to the top position by contracting your pecs, deltoids, and triceps. If needed, you can create extra resistance by adding weight plates to a belt or by placing a dumbbell between your calves.

FIRST PR ZONE (15 MINUTES)

A-2: CHINS (ON CHIN/DIP ASSIST UNIT)

Grasp a chinning bar with an underhand grip approximately shoulder width apart. From a hanging position, pull yourself up until your chin clears the bar. Reverse this motion to return to the starting position. Avoid flexing from the hips when performing pullups or chins.

This exercise is performed the same way as pullups, except that chins are performed with your palms facing toward you, which increases biceps involvement. The closer the grip, the more the biceps are involved. Chalk or lifting straps may be used to secure a good grip.

CHAPTER EIGHT

90 MINUTES PER WEEK

ONCE YOU'VE "CUT YOUR TEETH" ON THE EDT PROGRAMS FEATURED in Chapter Seven, it's time to graduate to more-demanding programs. The workouts in this chapter all feature two 15-minute PR Zones, for a total to 30 minutes per workout, excluding warmups. Most trainees will find these programs to be a perfect mix of effectiveness and time efficiency.

FIRST PR ZONE (15 MINUTES)

A-1: LONG STEP LUNGE (LEFT)

A-2: LONG STEP LUNGE (RIGHT)

With hands on hips, step forward with either leg. You will alternate legs each rep (for example, a total of 10 reps equals 1 set of 5). Keep your chest up, with your focus in front of you. Your rear heel will come up off of the floor as you sink down. When your rear knee lightly touches the floor, return to the starting position by pulling yourself back, letting your rear glute and hamstring muscles do the work. Use dumbbells for additional resistance when needed.

SECOND PR ZONE (15 MINUTES)

B-1: LOW CABLE ROW

Attach a straight bar to the low cable mechanism. Next, take a seated position with your feet on the bracing plates. Keeping both knees slightly bent, take an overhand grip on the bar and pull the handle to your lower abdomen. Reverse this motion to complete the rep. Maintain a fixed torso throughout, and be sure to actively squeeze your shoulder blades together at the completion of the pull.

SECOND PR ZONE (15 MINUTES)

B-2: FLAT DUMBBELL BENCH PRESS

The instability inherent in performing the bench press with dumbbells makes it more challenging than performing it with a barbell, because it requires much more balance and control. Carefully lie back on the bench with a dumbbell in each hand, allowing the dumbbells to move into the starting position. Press the dumbbells upward until your elbows are extended, but do not allow the dumbbells to touch at the top.

Always employ a competent spotter when performing any bench press variation.

EXITING THE BENCH AFTER A SET

There are two ways to exit the bench safely. If the dumbbells are light enough, you can return them to your thighs and roll forward to a seated position, and then stand up and return the dumbbells to their rack. However, if the dumbbells are too heavy, this won't be a viable option. In this case, under as much control as possible, lower the dumbbells one at a time to the floor. Do not lower them simultaneously, as this is likely to exceed the range of motion in your shoulder joints and cause injury.

Always employ a competent spotter when performing any bench press variation.

FIRST PR ZONE (15 MINUTES)

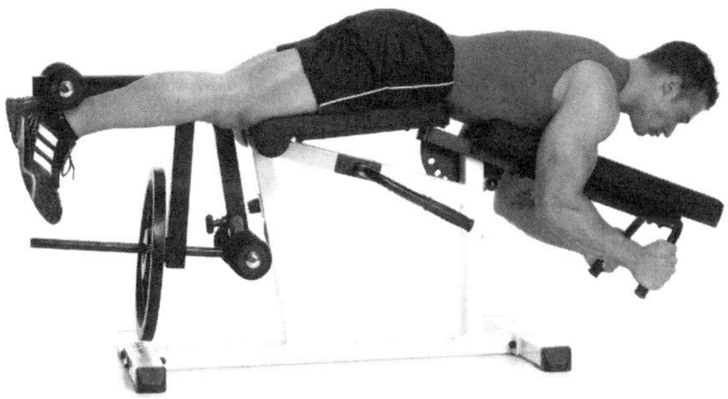

A-1: PRONE LEG CURL

The best leg curl machines feature a raised or arched bench, which facilitates a greater range of motion throughout the movement than a flat bench. Keep your head down and pelvis stabilized (or immobilized) during the movement. The knees should be aligned with the axis of the machine. If the roller behind the calves seems to slide up or down during the movement, adjust your alignment by sliding forward or back on the bench. Curl the weight by contracting the hamstrings. Pause at the top, and then lower yourself back to the starting position.

FIRST PR ZONE (15 MINUTES)

A-2: LEG EXTENSION

Position yourself on the seat of a leg extension machine and place your lower shins under the support pad or roller. From here, simply lift the weight by extending your knees. Return to the starting position. Be sure to keep your elbows stabilized (motionless) throughout the exercise.

SECOND PR ZONE (15 MINUTES)

B-1: STANDING HAMMER CURL

This is simply a standard curl performed with a thumbs-up grip, which increases the involvement of the brachialis muscle of the forearm. From a standing position, keep your elbows locked to your sides as you flex your elbows, maintaining a thumbs-up grip throughout. Return to the starting position, keeping your elbows stabilized (motionless) throughout the exercise.

FORM RECOMMENDATIONS FOR LOWER-BODY LIFTING

- Maintain the normal curvature of your lower back at all times. For example, if you're squatting or lifting a bar from the floor, don't allow your lower back to round. This is the cause of many avoidable lower-back injuries in the gym.
- Ensure and maintain left-right stance symmetry. Is your stance even, or is one foot more forward than the other? Is one foot turned out more than the other? If so, correct it.
- Ensure bar symmetry. When you squat or deadlift, is one end of the bar more forward than the other end? Or does one side of the bar dip lower than the other? This can indicate an imbalance—see if you can correct the situation by heightening your awareness of your body position.
- During squats, ensure that the bar is placed *below* the seventh cervical vertebra (if you reach back and feel the back of your neck, it's the vertebra that sticks out more than the others).
- Keep feet flat on the floor for all types of squats and deadlifts.

SECOND PR ZONE (15 MINUTES)

B-2: LYING DUMBBELL TRICEPS EXTENSION

Position yourself faceup on a bench or a Swiss ball. Using a pair of dumbbells, extend your arms until they are perpendicular to your torso. From this position, relax your triceps, and allow your elbows to flex until the dumbbells touch your shoulders. Return to the starting position, keeping your elbows stabilized (motionless) throughout the exercise.

FIRST PR ZONE (15 MINUTES)

A-1: BACK SQUAT

Position the barbell on the support pins inside a power rack so that the bar is level with your midchest. Place safety pins on each side at a position slightly lower than your intended deepest position. Place your hands evenly on the bar (a close grip with elbows under the bar will allow for a more upright posture), and, with your feet squarely under the bar, lift it from the rack by extending your legs.

Step back enough to avoid bumping the rack during the exercise, and position your feet shoulder width apart. The weight should remain centered over the back half of the feet, not on the heels or toes. Slowly descend into a near-bottom position, keeping the torso and back erect so that the hips remain under the bar. Do not allow the hips to drift backward or the torso to incline forward.

When viewed from the side, the angles formed at the knee joint and hip joint should be close to equal. Also, your hips and shoulders should ascend together—if the hips rise before the shoulders, it means you're using your back rather than your legs. Rise out of the squat following the same path that you descended—your torso and back erect and the hips under the bar throughout the ascent.

FIRST PR ZONE (15 MINUTES)

A-2: LAT PULLDOWN

Grasp the bar with your hands slightly wider than shoulder width apart, with palms facing away from your body. Next, pull the bar down toward your clavicle by contracting the latissimus dorsi ("lats") and elbow flexor muscles. Return to the starting position.

SECOND PR ZONE (15 MINUTES)

B-1: BACK EXTENSION

Perform this exercise by positioning yourself on a back extension machine. Adjust your position so that your hips are slightly forward of the support pad, which ensures that your pelvis can rotate during the exercise. Starting with the hips flexed at a 90-degree angle, raise yourself to a horizontal position by contracting the spinal erectors (lower-back muscles), glutes, and hamstrings. Pause, and lower yourself to the starting position.

SECOND PR ZONE (15 MINUTES)

B-2: FLAT DUMBBELL BENCH PRESS

The instability inherent in performing the bench press with dumbbells makes it more challenging than performing it with a barbell, because it requires much more balance and control. Carefully lie back on the bench with a dumbbell in each hand, allowing the dumbbells to move into the starting position. Press the dumbbells upward until your elbows are extended, but do not allow the dumbbells to touch at the top.

Always employ a competent spotter when performing any bench press variation.

FIRST PR ZONE (15 MINUTES)

A-1: LEG EXTENSION

Position yourself on the seat of a leg extension machine and place your lower shins under the support pad or roller. From here, simply lift the weight by extending your knees. Return to the starting position. Be sure to keep your elbows stabilized (motionless) throughout the exercise.

FIRST PR ZONE (15 MINUTES)

A-2: LYING DUMBBELL TRICEPS EXTENSION FROM FLOOR

Position yourself faceup while lying on the floor. Using a pair of dumbbells, extend your arms until they are perpendicular to your torso. From this position, relax your triceps, and allow your elbows to flex until the dumbbells touch your shoulders. Return to the starting position, keeping your elbows stabilized (motionless) throughout the exercise.

SECOND PR ZONE (15 MINUTES)

B-1: PLATE RAISE

From a standing position, grab a single weight plate with one hand on each side of the plate, as if they were on a steering wheel. Next, raise the plate in front of you until you can see through the hole. Pause for one second; then lower it under control. Complete the rep by reversing this position. Avoid resting the plate on your thighs between reps.

SECOND PR ZONE (15 MINUTES)

B-2: STRAIGHT-ARM PUSHDOWN

Stand in front of a lat pulldown bar with your arms outstretched toward the bar. Place your palms down flat on the bar. Keeping your elbows slightly bent, your wrists locked, and your torso erect, pull the bar down toward your body in an arcing motion until it contacts your thighs. To complete the rep, slowly allow the bar to come back up to the starting position.

FIRST PR ZONE (15 MINUTES)

A-1: PISTOL (RIGHT)

A-2: PISTOL (LEFT)

Directions for right side: **Stand in front of a bench, and extend both arms straight in front of you. Next, extend your left foot and leg so that your heel is just off the floor at all times. From this position, lower yourself to the bench under complete control by bending your right knee and keeping your support foot flat on the floor. Pause briefly and return to the starting position. Finish the reps on the right side, and then repeat the same motion for the reps on the left side.**

SECOND PR ZONE (15 MINUTES)

B-1: STANDING SINGLE-LEG CALF RAISE (LEFT)

B-2: STANDING SINGLE-LEG CALF RAISE (RIGHT)

Set the ball of one foot on a stable step or block at least 4 inches in height. Allow your heel to hang off of the block, and hold on to something (such as the vertical support of a squat cage) for balance. Lower your heel until you feel a significant stretch in your calf muscle, and then reverse this motion (by pushing away with your forefoot) to complete the rep.

FIRST PR ZONE (15 MINUTES)

A-1: DUMBBELL SHRUG

Take a standing position with a dumbbell in each hand, using a thumbs-forward hand position. From here, simply shrug your shoulders straight up. Complete the rep by reversing this motion.

FIRST PR ZONE (15 MINUTES)

A-2: DIPS (ON CHIN/DIP ASSIST UNIT)

Descend slowly and under complete control. Maintain a vertical torso for more shoulder and triceps involvement, and a forward lean to increase pectoral recruitment. Be careful not to exceed your shoulder's range of motion. Return back to the top position by contracting your pecs, deltoids, and triceps. If needed, you can create extra resistance by adding weight plates to a belt or by placing a dumbbell between your calves.

SECOND PR ZONE (15 MINUTES)

B-1: LOW CABLE BICEPS CURL

Attach a straight bar to a low pulley mechanism. Facing the cable unit in a standing position, keep your elbows pinned to your sides as you curl the bar. A slight rearward lean is permissible, but avoid hyperextending your lower back.

SECOND PR ZONE (15 MINUTES)

B-2: TRICEPS PUSHDOWN

This is performed from a high cable attachment, using either a straight bar or an E-Z curl bar. Grasp the handle and pull yourself into position, using your lats to extend your shoulders until your elbows are against your sides. From here, fully flex and extend your elbows while keeping your elbows pinned to your sides.

Note: With heavier weights, you may find it necessary to lean forward somewhat—athletes will also tend to place one foot ahead of the other to stabilize their position. With all triceps exercises, keep the backs of the wrists flat.

FIRST PR ZONE (15 MINUTES)

A-1: DUMBBELL THRUSTER

Assume a standing position with a dumbbell in each hand. Your arms should be in front of your torso as if you were simulating a boxer's guard position. Descend into a squat position. At the deepest point, the tops of your thighs should be parallel to the floor when viewed from the side. Immediately ascend, and as you reach a standing position, immediately and seamlessly press the dumbbells overhead with arms locked. Lower the dumbbells back to your shoulders.

Note: **There should not be a pause between the completion of the squat and the initiation of the dumbbell press—it should be a single continuous motion. Maintain an upright posture and neutral spine throughout. Do not pause between reps.**

FIRST PR ZONE (15 MINUTES)

A-2: STABILITY BALL CRUNCH

Sit on the ball, and "walk" forward until you're lying on the ball. Perform crunches in the normal manner, keeping in mind that a greater range of motion is achieved as the back drapes over the ball. The ball's instability and curved surface increase the level of difficulty of the crunch exercise while increasing the comfort of the movement.

During crunches, modify your arm position in order to adjust the level of resistance. The least resistance occurs when the arms are straight and outstretched along the side of the body during the movement. A more difficult variation is to cross the arms against the chest. The most difficult variation is to place the hands such that the fingers are touching the head at a point just behind the ears. Avoid interlacing the fingers and clasping them behind the head, which can strain the cervical vertebrae and encourage participation from other muscles.

Additional resistance (in the form of a medicine ball or a weight plate) can be used when body weight is no longer sufficient to cause an improvement in strength. When using additional resistance, it becomes necessary to anchor the feet under an immovable object to stabilize position.

SECOND PR ZONE (15 MINUTES)

B-1: 45-DEGREE FRONT DUMBBELL RAISE

Grab a pair of dumbbells and take a seated position on an incline bench with arms straight and at your sides, thumbs facing in (reverse grip). Keeping your elbows straight, raise the dumbbells up and forward until your hands are at about eye level. Keep the backs of your wrists flat and elbows straight throughout. Complete the rep by reversing this motion.

SECOND PR ZONE (15 MINUTES)

B-2: STANDING TWO-ARM TRICEPS KICKBACK

Assume a standing position with a light dumbbell in each hand. Lean forward from the hips and pull the dumbbells toward your armpits as you raise your elbows as high as comfort allows. From this position, simply "kick" the dumbbells back behind you by extending your elbows. Once your arms have reached a locked-out position behind you, complete the rep by reversion this motion.

FIRST PR ZONE (15 MINUTES)

A-1: STIFF-LEG DEADLIFT

Set up a barbell at slightly higher than knee level (use a power rack, or set the barbell on blocks). Using an overhand grip, grab the bar with a shoulder-width grip, and step back just enough to clear the rack. Inhale, slightly bend the knees, and begin the movement while maintaining your body weight over your heels. Allow the bar to descend while you ensure it maintains contact with the front of your body. While descending, maintain the normal curvature of the lower back and the neck, and allow the glutes to move rearward. Do not look up, but instead, maintain a normal head and neck alignment. Always use a controlled-movement speed with this exercise. Never perform it rapidly or explosively.

A-2: BARBELL ROLLOUT

Load a barbell to 95 pounds (using a 25-pound plate on each end). Kneel in front of the barbell and grasp it with a shoulder-width overhand grip. Keeping your arms straight, roll the bar out to the front as you lower your trunk toward the floor. Complete the rep by pulling yourself back to the starting position.

SECOND PR ZONE (15 MINUTES)

B-1: SEATED DUMBBELL REVERSE CURL

Grab a pair of dumbbells and sit at the end of a bench with arms straight and at your sides, thumbs facing in (reverse grip). Keeping your elbows pinned to your sides, curl the dumbbells up by flexing your elbows. Keep the backs of your wrists flat throughout. Complete the rep by reversing this motion.

SECOND PR ZONE (15 MINUTES)

B-2: SEATED DUMBBELL MILITARY PRESS

Grab a pair of dumbbells and take a seated position on a bench. Hold the dumbbells at the edges of your shoulders, with palms facing forward. Next, press the dumbbells directly upward until your arms are locked out overhead. In the top position, the dumbbells should be close to each other but not touching. Complete the rep by reversing this motion.

FIRST PR ZONE (15 MINUTES)

A-1: PUSH PRESS

Place a loaded bar on a rack at about your upper-chest level. Grasping the bar with both hands, lift it off the rack and support it on your shoulders. Dip the body by bending the knees, hips, and ankles slightly. Explosively drive upward with the legs, driving the barbell up off the shoulders, vigorously extending arms overhead until your elbows are locked. Reverse this motion to complete the rep.

FIRST PR ZONE (15 MINUTES)

A-2: CHINS

Grasp a chinning bar with an underhand grip, approximately shoulder width apart. From a hanging position, pull yourself up until your chin clears the bar. Reverse this motion to return to the starting position. Avoid flexing from the hips when performing pullups or chins.

This exercise is performed the same way as pullups, except that chins are performed with your palms facing toward you, which increases biceps involvement. The closer the grip, the more the biceps are involved. Chalk or lifting straps may be used to secure a good grip.

SECOND PR ZONE (15 MINUTES)

B-1: STEPUP (LEFT)

B-2: STEPUP (RIGHT)

Perform these on a 14- to 16-inch bench or block. As you step up, keep the stress on the quads by making sure that the nonworking foot never rests on the floor. Also make sure that your working knee stays directly over the middle of the working foot. Complete all reps for first leg, rest, and complete reps for the opposite leg.

FIRST PR ZONE (15 MINUTES)

A-1: BENCH PRESS

Lie faceup on the bench, placing both feet on the floor. Grasp the bar such that both hands are equidistant from the center, and make sure your thumbs are wrapped around the bar, rather than on the same side as your other fingers. At the start, the bar should be directly over your nose—if it isn't, slide yourself up or down on the bench until it is. Inhale, and unrack the bar from the supports. As you lower the bar to your chest, keep your elbows directly under the bar, rather than in front of or ahead of the bar. At the bottom of the movement, the bar should lightly touch your chest at nipple level. Return the bar to the starting position (it should actually travel up, as well as slightly back) by contracting your pectorals.

Always employ a competent spotter when performing any bench press variation.

FIRST PR ZONE (15 MINUTES)

A-2: LOW CABLE ROW

Attach a straight bar to the low cable mechanism. Next, take a seated position with your feet on the bracing plates. Keeping both knees slightly bent, take an overhand grip on the bar and pull the handle to your lower abdomen. Reverse this motion to complete the rep. Maintain a fixed torso throughout, and be sure to actively squeeze your shoulder blades together at the completion of the pull.

SECOND PR ZONE (15 MINUTES)

B-1: SUPINE LEG CURL

Lying faceup on the floor, position your heels on the ball and pull your toes up toward your shins as you pull your shoulder blades back and down. Contract your gluteals until your body is in a straight line from ankle to shoulder. Keeping your hips tall, pull your heels in toward your gluteals. Let the ball roll back slowly as you straighten your legs. Keep your hips elevated for all repetitions.

SECOND PR ZONE (15 MINUTES)

B-2: HACK SQUAT, FROM TOES

Position yourself under the hack squat machine's shoulder supports, and place your feet symmetrically on the foot platform. In this variation of the exercise, you'll keep your heels about ½ inch away from the foot plate throughout.

Once you've established your position on the machine, disengage the safety mechanism, and descend into a semisquat by flexing at your hips and knees. Complete the rep by returning to the starting position. Make sure to reengage the safety mechanism before exiting the machine.

FIRST PR ZONE (15 MINUTES)

A-1: DUMBBELL SNATCH (LEFT)

A-2: DUMBBELL SNATCH (RIGHT)

Begin by squatting low over a dumbbell. Maintain a locked and rigid lower back. The feet should be about shoulder width apart. Grasp the dumbbell and tighten the abdominal muscles. In an explosive and continuous motion, accelerate the dumbbell upward until your arm is straight and locked. The dumbbell should travel close to the body and not swing out or away. Briefly hold it above the head, and then bring it down to the starting position. If necessary, you may assist the descent by using the opposite hand.

SECOND PR ZONE (15 MINUTES)

B-1: SINGLE-ARM DUMBBELL MILITARY PRESS (LEFT)

B-2: SINGLE-ARM DUMBBELL MILITARY PRESS (RIGHT)

Raise a single dumbbell to shoulder height. The dumbbell should start at the edge of your same-side shoulder, with palm facing forward. Hold on to something with your free hand to stabilize yourself. Lock your legs and hips. Keep your elbow in and your palm forward as you press the dumbbell straight up to arm's length. Complete the rep by reversing this motion.

FIRST PR ZONE (15 MINUTES)

A-1: FLAT DUMBBELL BENCH PRESS

The instability inherent in performing the bench press with dumbbells makes it more challenging than performing it with a barbell, because it requires much more balance and control. Carefully lie back on the bench with a dumbbell in each hand, allowing the dumbbells to move into the starting position. Press the dumbbells upward until your elbows are extended, but do not allow the dumbbells to touch at the top.

Always employ a competent spotter when performing any bench press variation.

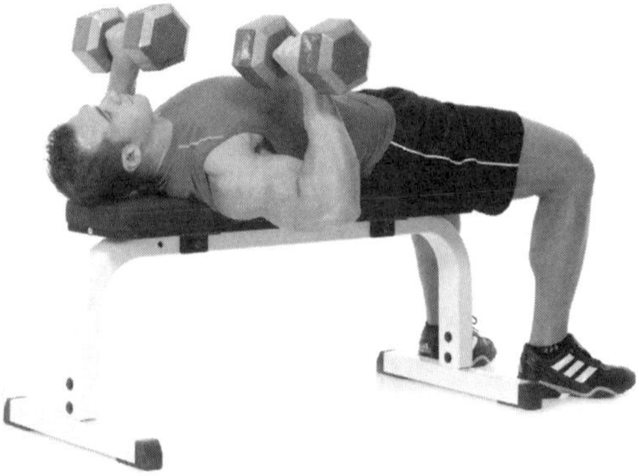

A-2: LOW CABLE ROW (WIDE GRIP)

Attach a straight bar to the low cable mechanism. Next, take a seated position with your feet on the bracing plates. Keeping both knees slightly bent, take a wider-than-shoulder-width overhand grip on the bar, and pull the handle to your lower abdomen. Reverse this motion to complete the rep. Maintain a fixed torso throughout, and be sure to actively squeeze your shoulder blades together at the completion of the pull.

SECOND PR ZONE (15 MINUTES)

B-1: 45-DEGREE-INCLINE DUMBBELL REVERSE CURL

Grab a pair of dumbbells and take a seated position on an incline bench. With arms straight and at your sides, thumbs facing in (reverse grip), and keeping your elbows pinned to your sides, curl the dumbbells up by flexing your elbows. Keep the backs of your wrists flat throughout. Complete the rep by reversing this motion.

SECOND PR ZONE (15 MINUTES)

B-2: PUSHUP

Pushups are basically a form of bench pressing without the bench. Keep your hands slightly wider than shoulder width apart, and maintain a straight and rigid torso as you lower your chest to the ground. The difficulty of this exercise may be increased by elevating your feet (on a bench, for example).

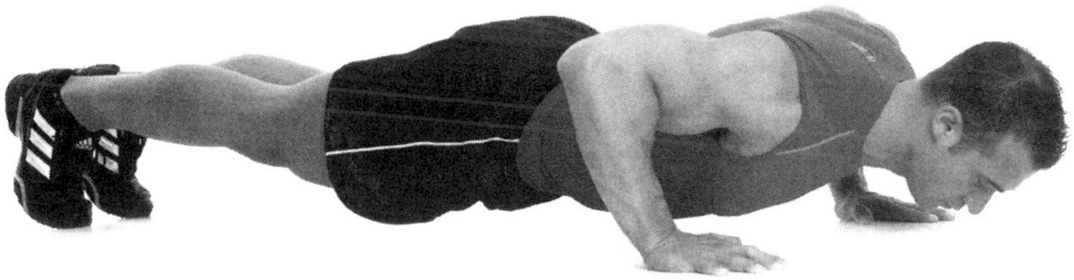

CHAPTER NINE

135 MINUTES PER WEEK

IN SOME CASES, TRAINEES MAY REQUIRE HIGHER TRAINING VOLUMES in order to make continued progress. The programs in this chapter all consist of three 15-minute PR Zones, or a total of 45 minutes of training three times per week. Compared with more conventional styles of resistance training, these workouts are still rather brief. However, due to the efficiency of the EDT system, you'll find these workouts truly challenging. Unless you're already highly conditioned, spend several weeks on the shorter training cycles presented in Chapters Seven and Eight before graduating to these programs.

FIRST PR ZONE (15 MINUTES)

A-1: CHINS (ON CHIN/DIP ASSIST UNIT)

Grasp a chinning bar with an underhand grip approximately shoulder width apart. From a hanging position, pull yourself up until your chin clears the bar. Reverse this motion to return to the starting position. Avoid flexing from the hips when performing pullups or chins.

This exercise is performed the same way as pullups, except that chins are performed with your palms facing toward you, which increases biceps involvement. The closer the grip, the more the biceps are involved. Chalk or lifting straps may be used to secure a good grip.

A-2: MILITARY PRESS

Place a loaded bar on a rack at about your upper-chest level. Grasping the bar with both hands, lift it off the rack, and support it on your shoulders. Then, with the strength of the shoulders and triceps, press the bar upward until it is directly overhead, with both arms extended and locked at the elbows. Return to the starting position to complete the rep.

SECOND PR ZONE (15 MINUTES)

B-1: DRAG CURL

Drag curls are used to concentrate muscular stress on the outer portion of the biceps. This isolated exercise results in greater development of your outer biceps, which tends to create a more defined separation between your biceps and triceps muscles.

Starting from the same initial position for standard barbell curls, hold the bar with both arms extended downward, gripping the bar with your palms facing up. Lift the bar, but instead of keeping both elbows locked to your side and lifting it in an arc, allow both elbows to move backward in order to "drag" the bar in a straight line directly up the front of your body. Once the bar reaches your lower-chest area, reverse this motion to complete the rep.

SECOND PR ZONE (15 MINUTES)

B-2: STANDING LATERAL RAISE

Begin this exercise from a standing position with a dumbbell in each hand. Maintaining an upright posture (think: "Chest up!"), raise the dumbbells up to your sides until your arms are parallel to the ground. Reverse this motion to complete the rep.

THIRD PR ZONE (15 MINUTES)

C-1: TRICEPS PUSHDOWN

This is performed from a high cable attachment, using either a straight bar or an E-Z curl bar. Grasp the handle and pull yourself into position, using your lats to extend your shoulders until your elbows are against your sides. From here, fully flex and extend your elbows while keeping them pinned to your sides.

Note: With heavier weights, you may find it necessary to lean forward somewhat—athletes will also tend to place one foot ahead of the other to stabilize their position. With all triceps exercises, keep the backs of the wrists flat.

THIRD PR ZONE (15 MINUTES)

C-2: BARBELL SHRUG

Position the barbell on a rack at approximately knee level. Facing the bar, grasp it and lift it off the rack, stepping backward just enough to clear the rack. From this position, simply shrug your shoulders straight up toward your ears and back down, keeping your arms straight and the bar next to your body.

FIRST PR ZONE (15 MINUTES)

A-1: STEPUP (LEFT)

A-2: STEPUP (RIGHT)

Perform these on a 14- to 16-inch bench or block. As you step up, keep the stress on the quads by making sure that the nonworking foot never rests on the floor. Your working knee should stay directly over the middle of the working foot. Complete all reps for first leg, rest, and complete reps for the opposite leg.

SECOND PR ZONE (15 MINUTES)

B-1: BACK EXTENSION

Perform this exercise by positioning yourself on a back extension machine. Adjust your position so that your hips are slightly forward of the support pad, which ensures that your pelvis can rotate during the exercise. Starting with the hips flexed at a 90-degree angle, raise yourself to a horizontal position by contracting the spinal erectors (lower-back muscles), glutes, and hamstrings. Pause, and then lower yourself to the starting position.

SECOND PR ZONE (15 MINUTES)

B-2: HANGING KNEE-UP

Hanging from an overhead support, start with the entire body fully extended. Flex at the hips and knees simultaneously until the tops of the thighs are parallel to the floor. Relax and return to the starting position.

THIRD PR ZONE (15 MINUTES)

C-1: SEATED CALF RAISE

Position yourself on a bench with the balls of your feet resting on a 4- to 6-inch step. Let your heels rest just above the ground. Resting two dumbbells of moderate weight just above your knees, push upward by contracting your calves. Return to the starting position to complete the rep.

THIRD PR ZONE (15 MINUTES)

C-2: STABILITY BALL CRUNCH

Sit on the ball, and "walk" forward until you're lying on the ball. Perform crunches in the normal manner, keeping in mind that a greater range of motion is achieved as the back drapes over the ball. The ball's instability and curved surface increase the level of difficulty of the crunch exercise while increasing the comfort of the movement.

During crunches, modify arm position in order to adjust the level of resistance. The least resistance occurs when the arms are straight and outstretched along the side of the body during the movement. A more difficult variation is to cross the arms against the chest. The most difficult variation is to place the hands such that the fingers are touching the head at a point just behind the ears. Avoid interlacing the fingers and clasping them behind the head, which can strain the cervical vertebrae and encourage participation from other muscles.

Additional resistance (in the form of a medicine ball or a weight plate) can be used when body weight is no longer sufficient to cause an improvement in strength. When using additional resistance, it becomes necessary to anchor the feet under an immovable object to stabilize your position.

FIRST PR ZONE (15 MINUTES)

A-1: DIPS (ON CHIN/DIP-ASSIST UNIT)

Descend slowly and under complete control. Maintain a vertical torso for more shoulder and triceps involvement, and a forward lean to increase pectoral recruitment. Be careful not to exceed your shoulder's range of motion. Return back to the top position by contracting your pecs, deltoids, and triceps. If needed, you can create extra resistance by adding weight plates to a belt or by placing a dumbbell between your calves.

FIRST PR ZONE (15 MINUTES)

A-2: CHINS (ON CHIN/DIP-ASSIST UNIT)

Grasp a chinning bar with an underhand grip approximately shoulder width apart. From a hanging position, pull yourself up until your chin clears the bar. Reverse this motion to return to the starting position. Avoid flexing from the hips when performing pullups or chins.

This exercise is performed the same way as pullups, except that chins are performed with your palms facing toward you, which increases biceps involvement. The closer the grip, the more the biceps are involved. Chalk or lifting straps may be used to secure a good grip.

SECOND PR ZONE (15 MINUTES)

B-1: LEG EXTENSION

Position yourself on the seat of the leg extension machine and place your lower shins under the support pad or roller. From here, simply lift the weight by extending your knees. Return to the starting position. Be sure to keep your elbows stabilized (motionless) throughout the exercise.

SECOND PR ZONE (15 MINUTES)

B-2: PRONE LEG CURL

The best leg curl machines feature a raised or arched bench, which facilitates a greater range of motion throughout the movement, as opposed to a flat bench. Keep your head down and pelvis stabilized (or immobilized) during the movement. The knees should be aligned with the axis of the machine. If the roller behind the calves seems to slide up or down during the movement, adjust your alignment by sliding forward or back on the bench. Curl the weight by contracting the hamstrings. Pause at the top, and then lower yourself to the starting position.

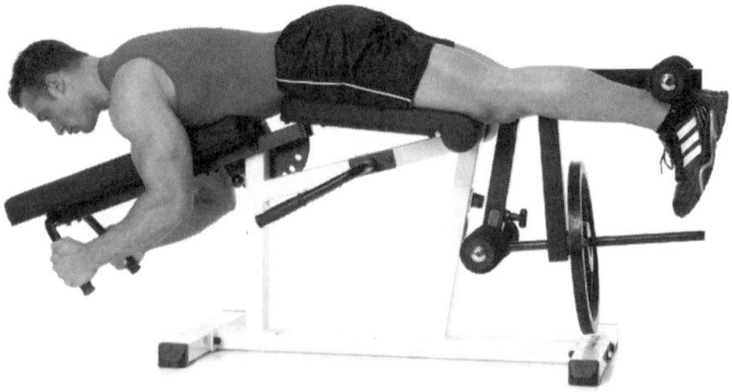

THIRD PR ZONE (15 MINUTES)

C-1: 45-DEGREE-INCLINE HAMMER CURL

Grab a pair of dumbbells and take a seated position on an incline bench, with arms straight and on the support pad, thumbs facing forward (hammer grip). Keeping your elbows stationary, curl the dumbbells up by flexing your elbows as shown. Keep the backs of your wrists flat throughout. Complete the rep by reversing this motion.

THIRD PR ZONE (15 MINUTES)

C-2: REVERSE-GRIP TRICEPS EXTENSION

This is performed from a high cable attachment, using either a straight bar or an E-Z curl bar. Grasp the handle with a palms-up grip and pull yourself into position, using your lats to extend your shoulders until your elbows are against your sides. From here, fully flex and extend your elbows while keeping your elbows pinned to your sides. With heavier weights, it will become necessary to lean forward somewhat—athletes will also tend to place one foot ahead of the other to stabilize their position.

***Note:* With all triceps exercises, keep the back of the wrists flat.**

FIRST PR ZONE (15 MINUTES)

A-1: LEG PRESS (FROM TOES ONLY, HEELS SLIGHTLY OFF THE PLATFORM)

Assume a seated position on the leg press machine with feet about shoulder width apart on the foot plate. Keep your lower back flat against the seat back at all times. Straighten your legs and release the safety mechanism (see the machine's instruction card for more details). Lift your heels about ½ inch off the foot plate (this maneuver increases the contribution of your quadriceps muscles and decreases the involvement of the hamstrings), and lower the foot plate toward you, allowing it to descend as much as you can without rounding your lower back. Pause; then push the foot plate back to the top position.

FIRST PR ZONE (15 MINUTES)

A-2: BACK EXTENSION

Perform this exercise by positioning yourself on a back extension machine. Adjust your position so that your hips are slightly forward of the support pad, which ensures that your pelvis can rotate during the exercise. Starting with the hips flexed at a 90-degree angle, raise yourself to a horizontal position by contracting the spinal erectors (lower-back muscles), glutes, and hamstrings. Pause, and lower yourself to the starting position.

SECOND PR ZONE (15 MINUTES)

B-1: BULGARIAN SPLIT SQUAT (LEFT)

B-2: BULGARIAN SPLIT SQUAT (RIGHT)

With your back foot resting on a bench, lower your body until the knee of your rear leg almost touches the floor. Pause; then raise yourself until your front knee is nearly straight. Maintain an upright torso throughout.

THIRD PR ZONE (15 MINUTES)

C-1:
CONCENTRATION CURL (LEFT)

C-2:
CONCENTRATION CURL (RIGHT)

Sit sideways on a bench and grasp a dumbbell between your feet. Place the back of your upper arm to your inner thigh for support. From this position, curl the dumbbell to the front of your same-side shoulder. Complete the rep by reversing this motion.

FIRST PR ZONE (15 MINUTES)

A-1: LOW CABLE ROW

Attach a straight bar to the low cable mechanism. Next, take a seated position with your feet on the bracing plates. Keeping both knees slightly bent, take an overhand grip on the bar and pull the handle to your lower abdomen. Reverse this motion to complete the rep. Maintain a fixed torso throughout, and be sure to actively squeeze your shoulder blades together at the completion of the pull.

FIRST PR ZONE (15 MINUTES)

A-2: 45-DEGREE-INCLINE BARBELL PRESS

Assume a seated position on an incline bench with a loaded barbell in the supports. Grasping the bar with your hands slightly wider than shoulder width apart, remove the bar from its supports and, keeping your arms straight, carefully shift the bar away from the rack. Next, lower the bar to your upper chest. Pause slightly, and complete the rep by pushing the bar straight up until your arms are completely straight. Keep your butt and lower back against the bench, and keep both feet on the floor at all times.

SECOND PR ZONE (15 MINUTES)

B-1: SEATED PRESS (ALSO CALLED A SEATED DUMBBELL OVERHEAD PRESS)

Grab a pair of dumbbells and assume a seated position on a bench. Hold the dumbbells at the edges of your shoulders with your palms facing forward. Next, press the dumbbells straight up and slightly inward until your arms reach a locked-out position overhead. Complete the rep by reversing this motion.

SECOND PR ZONE (15 MINUTES)

B-2: BARBELL CURL

From a standing position, extend both arms downward and grasp the bar with a palms-up grip. Without moving at the shoulders, and with each elbow locked firmly in place, flex both arms at the elbows, raising the bar in an upward arc until both arms are completely flexed with the bar pressed against your chest. The bar is then lowered through the same arcing path to complete the rep.

THIRD PR ZONE (15 MINUTES)

C-1: TRICEPS PUSHDOWN

This is performed from a high cable attachment, using either a straight bar or an E-Z curl bar. Grasp the handle and pull yourself into position, using your lats to extend your shoulders until your elbows are against your sides. From here, fully flex and extend your elbows while keeping your elbows pinned to your sides.

Note: With heavier weights, you may find it necessary to lean forward somewhat—athletes will also tend to place one foot ahead of the other to stabilize their position. With all triceps exercises, keep the backs of the wrists flat.

THIRD PR ZONE (15 MINUTES)

C-2: BARBELL REVERSE CURL

From a standing position, extend both arms downward and grasp the bar with a palms-down grip. Without moving at the shoulders and with each elbow locked firmly in place, flex both arms at the elbows, raising the bar in an arc until both arms are completely flexed with the bar pressed against your chest. The bar is then lowered through the same arcing path to complete the rep.

FIRST PR ZONE (15 MINUTES)

A-1: HACK SQUAT

Position yourself under the hack squat machine's shoulder supports and place your feet symmetrically on the platform. Keep in mind that a higher foot placement intensifies the training stress on the glutes and hamstrings (especially if you push from the heels), while a relatively lower foot placement tends to throw the brunt of the load on your quadriceps (especially if you push from your forefoot).

Once you've established your position on the machine, disengage the safety mechanism, and descend into a semisquat by flexing at your hips and knees. Complete the rep by returning to the starting position. Make sure to reengage the safety mechanism before exiting the machine.

A-2: PRONE LEG CURL

The best leg curl machines feature a raised or arched bench, which facilitates a greater range of motion throughout the movement, as opposed to a flat bench. Keep your head down and pelvis stabilized (or immobilized) during the movement. The knees should be aligned with the axis of the machine. If the roller behind the calves seems to slide up or down during the movement, adjust your alignment by sliding forward or back on the bench. Curl the weight by contracting the hamstrings. Pause at the top, and then lower yourself to the starting position.

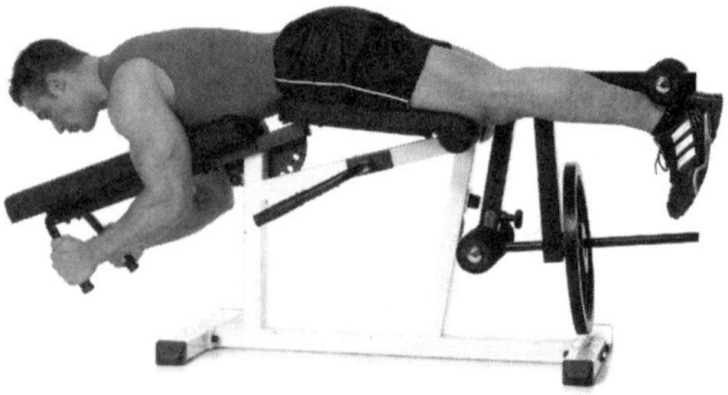

SECOND PR ZONE (15 MINUTES)

B-1: SEATED CALF RAISE

Position yourself on a bench with the balls of your feet resting on a 4- to 6-inch step. Let your heels rest just above the ground. Resting two dumbbells of moderate weight just above your knees, push upward by contracting your calves. Return to the starting position to complete the rep.

SECOND PR ZONE (15 MINUTES)

B-2: STABILITY BALL CRUNCH

Sit on the ball, and "walk" forward until you're lying on the ball. Perform crunches in the normal manner, keeping in mind that a greater range of motion is achieved as the back drapes over the ball. The ball's instability and curved surface increase the level of difficulty of the crunch exercise while increasing the comfort of the movement.

During crunches, modify arm position in order to adjust the level of resistance. The least resistance occurs when the arms are straight and outstretched along the side of the body during the movement. A more difficult variation is to cross the arms against the chest. The most difficult variation is to place the hands such that the fingers are touching the head at a point just behind the ears. Avoid interlacing the fingers and clasping them behind the head, which can strain the cervical vertebrae and encourage participation from other muscles.

Additional resistance (in the form of a medicine ball or a weight plate) can be used when body weight is no longer sufficient to cause an improvement in strength. When using additional resistance, it becomes necessary to anchor the feet under an immovable object to stabilize position.

THIRD PR ZONE (15 MINUTES)

C-1: SEATED CALF RAISE

Position yourself on a bench with the balls of your feet resting on a 4- to 6-inch step. Let your heels rest just above the ground. Resting two dumbbells of moderate weight just above your knees, push upward by contracting your calves. Return to the starting position to complete the rep.

THIRD PR ZONE (15 MINUTES)

C-2: HANGING KNEE-UP

Hanging from an overhead support, start with the entire body fully extended. Flex at the hips and knees simultaneously until the tops of the thighs are parallel to the floor. Relax and return to the starting position.

FIRST PR ZONE (15 MINUTES)

A-1: BULGARIAN SPLIT SQUAT (LEFT)

A-2: BULGARIAN SPLIT SQUAT (RIGHT)

With your back foot resting on a bench, lower your body until the knee of your rear leg almost touches the floor. Pause; then raise yourself until your front knee is nearly straight. Maintain an upright torso throughout.

SECOND PR ZONE (15 MINUTES)

B-1: 45-DEGREE-INCLINE BARBELL PRESS

Assume a seated position on an incline bench with a loaded barbell in the supports. Grasping the bar with your hands slightly wider than shoulder width apart, remove the bar from its supports and, keeping your arms straight, carefully shift the bar away from the rack. Next, lower the bar to your upper chest. Pause slightly, and complete the rep by pushing the bar straight up until your arms are completely straight. Keep your butt and lower back against the bench, and keep both feet on the floor at all times.

SECOND PR ZONE (15 MINUTES)

B-2: BENT BARBELL ROW

Stand with feet shoulder width apart and bend forward at the waist, pushing your hips back and keeping your knees slightly flexed. Keep your lower back in its normal arched position throughout (when viewed from the side, your torso should be at about a 45-degree angle to the floor during this exercise). From here, grasp a loaded barbell with an overhand shoulder-width grip. Next, pull the bar to your lower sternum, and squeeze your shoulder blades together at the top of the pull. Complete the rep by reversing this action.

THIRD PR ZONE (15 MINUTES)

C-1: PREACHER HAMMER CURL

Leaning over a stability ball, grasp two dumbbells of moderate weight. Keeping your upper arms at a 45-degree angle, curl the weights up until your forearms are just short of being perpendicular to the floor. Complete the rep by reversing this action.

THIRD PR ZONE (15 MINUTES)

C-2: LYING DUMBBELL TRICEPS EXTENSION

Position yourself faceup on a bench or a Swiss ball. Using a pair of dumbbells, extend your arms until they are perpendicular to your torso. From this position, relax your triceps and allow your elbows to flex until the dumbbells touch your shoulders. Return to the starting position, keeping your elbows stabilized (motionless) throughout the exercise.

PROGRAM #4
135 MIN
SESSION 2

FIRST PR ZONE (15 MINUTES)

A-1: LONG STEP LUNGE (LEFT)
A-2: LONG STEP LUNGE (RIGHT)

With hands on hips, step forward with either leg. You will alternate legs each rep (for example, a total of 10 reps equals 1 set of 5). Keep your chest up with your focus in front of you. Your rear heel will come up off of the floor as you sink down. When your rear knee lightly touches the floor, return to the starting position by pulling yourself back, letting your rear glute and hamstring muscles do the work. Use dumbbells for additional resistance when needed.

SECOND PR ZONE (15 MINUTES)

B-1: BENCH PRESS

Lie faceup on the bench, placing both feet on the floor. Grasp the bar such that both hands are equidistant from the center, and make sure your thumbs are wrapped around the bar, rather than on the same side as your other fingers. At the start, the bar should be directly over your nose—if it isn't, slide yourself up or down on the bench until it is. Inhale, and unrack the bar from the supports. As you lower the bar to your chest, keep your elbows directly under the bar, rather than in front of or ahead of the bar. At the bottom of the movement, the bar should lightly touch your chest at nipple level. Return the bar to the starting position (it should actually travel up, as well as slightly back) by contracting your pectorals.

Always employ a competent spotter when performing any bench press variation.

SECOND PR ZONE (15 MINUTES)

B-2: CLOSE-GRIP LAT PULLDOWN

Grasp the triangle handle that is attached to the high pulley mechanism of a lat-pulldown machine. Next, position your knees under the machine's supports and pull the handle down toward your clavicles by contracting the lats and elbow flexor muscles. Complete the rep by reversing this action.

THIRD PR ZONE (15 MINUTES)

C-1: 45-DEGREE-INCLINE DUMBBELL CURL

Grab a pair of dumbbells and take a seated position on an incline bench. Your arms should hang straight down at your sides, thumbs facing out (reverse grip). Keeping your elbows pinned to your sides, curl the dumbbells up by flexing your elbows as shown. Keep the backs of your wrists flat throughout. Complete the rep by reversing this motion.

THIRD PR ZONE (15 MINUTES)

C-2: TRICEPS EXTENSION WITH TRICEPS ROPE

This is performed from a high cable attachment, using a triceps rope attachment. Grasp the rope and pull yourself into position, using your lats to extend your shoulders until your elbows are against your sides. From here, fully flex and extend your elbows while keeping your elbows pinned to your sides. With heavier weights, it will become necessary to lean forward somewhat—athletes will also tend to place one foot ahead of the other to stabilize their position.

Note: **With all triceps exercises, keep the backs of your wrists flat.**

FIRST PR ZONE (15 MINUTES)

A-1: BENCH PRESS

Lie faceup on the bench, placing both feet on the floor. Grasp the bar such that both hands are equidistant from the center, and make sure your thumbs are wrapped around the bar, rather than on the same side as your other fingers. At the start, the bar should be directly over your nose—if it isn't, slide yourself up or down on the bench until it is. Inhale, and unrack the bar from the supports. As you lower the bar to your chest, keep your elbows directly under the bar, rather than in front of or ahead of the bar. At the bottom of the movement, the bar should lightly touch your chest at nipple level. Return the bar to the starting position (it should actually travel up, as well as slightly back) by contracting your pectorals.

Always employ a competent spotter when performing any bench press variation.

FIRST PR ZONE (15 MINUTES)

A-2: PULLUP (ON CHIN/DIP ASSIST UNIT)

Grasp a chinning bar with an overhand grip approximately shoulder distance in width. From a hanging position, pull yourself up until your chin clears the bar. Reverse this motion to return to the starting position. Avoid flexing from the hips when performing pullups or chins.

SECOND PR ZONE (15 MINUTES)

B-1: 45-DEGREE-INCLINE BARBELL PRESS

Assume a seated position on an incline bench with a loaded barbell in the supports. Grasping the bar with your hands slightly wider than shoulderwidth apart, remove the bar from its supports and, keeping your arms straight, carefully shift the bar away from the rack. Next, lower the bar to your upper chest. Pause slightly, and complete the rep by pushing the bar straight up until your arms are completely straight. Keep your butt and lower back against the bench, and keep both feet on the floor at all times.

SECOND PR ZONE (15 MINUTES)

B-2: LOW CABLE ROW

Attach a straight bar to the low cable mechanism. Next, take a seated position with your feet on the bracing plates. Keeping both knees slightly bent, take an overhand grip on the bar and pull the handle to your lower abdomen. Reverse this motion to complete the rep. Maintain a fixed torso throughout, and be sure to actively squeeze your shoulder blades together at the completion of the pull.

THIRD PR ZONE (15 MINUTES)

C-1: STANDING BARBELL CURL

From a standing position, extend both arms downward and grasp the bar with a palms-up grip. Without moving at the shoulders and with each elbow locked firmly in place, flex both arms at the elbows, raising the bar in an arc until both arms are completely flexed, with the bar pressed against your chest. The bar is then lowered through the same arcing path to complete the rep.

THIRD PR ZONE (15 MINUTES)

C-2: STANDING BARBELL MILITARY PRESS

Place a loaded bar on a rack at about your upper-chest level. Grasping the bar with both hands, lift it off the rack and support it on your shoulders as shown. From this position, drive the barbell up off the shoulders, vigorously extending arms overhead until your elbows are locked. Keep your back and legs locked throughout. Reverse this motion to complete the rep.

FIRST PR ZONE (15 MINUTES)

A-1: SINGLE-LEG EXTENSION (LEFT)

A-2: SINGLE-LEG LEG EXTENSION (RIGHT)

Sit on the leg extension machine with the undersides of your knees firmly braced against the forward edge of the seat. Place your feet under the machine's footpad or roller. From here extend one knee until your leg is completely straight. Pause, and complete the rep by reversing this action.

SECOND PR ZONE (15 MINUTES)

B-1: SUPINE LEG CURL

Lying faceup on the floor, position your heels on the ball and pull your toes up toward your shins as you pull your shoulder blades back and down. Contract your gluteals until your body is in a straight line from ankle to shoulder. Keeping your hips tall, pull your heels in toward your gluteals. Let the ball roll back slowly as you straighten your legs. Keep your hips elevated for all repetitions.

SECOND PR ZONE (15 MINUTES)

B-2: SQUAT

Position the barbell on the support pins inside of a power rack so that the bar is level with your midchest. Place safety pins on each side, at a position slightly lower than your intended deepest position. Place your hands evenly on the bar (a close grip with elbows under the bar will allow for a more upright posture). With your feet squarely under the bar, lift it from the rack by extending your legs.

Next, step back just enough to avoid bumping the rack during the exercise, and position your feet at approximately shoulder width. The weight should remain centered over the back half of your feet, not on the heels or toes. Slowly descend into a near-bottom position, keeping the torso and back erect so that the hips remain under the bar at all times. Do not allow the hips to drift backward or the torso to drift forward. Rise out of the squat position, following the same path that you descended. Your torso and back should remain erect, and your hips should remain under the bar throughout the ascent.

THIRD PR ZONE (15 MINUTES)

C-1: HIGH CABLE CRUNCH

Stand with a rope attached to a high-cable pulley, feet hip width apart, knees slightly bent. Facing away from the machine, grasp the rope with both hands at forehead height, elbows bent, upper arms parallel to floor and each other. Maintaining arm position, flex forward in a crunch motion without changing hip angle. Complete the rep by reversing this action.

Note: **If you're performing this at a lat pulldown station, you can stabilize yourself by pinching the seat with your legs.**

THIRD PR ZONE (15 MINUTES)

C-2: SEATED CALF RAISE

Position yourself on a bench with the balls of your feet resting on a 4- to 6-inch step. Let your heels rest just above the ground. Resting two dumbbells of moderate weight just above your knees, push upward by contracting your calves. Return to the starting position to complete the rep.

FIRST PR ZONE (15 MINUTES)

A-1: BENCH PRESS

Lie faceup on the bench, placing both feet on the floor. Grasp the bar such that both hands are equidistant from the center, and make sure your thumbs are wrapped around the bar, rather than on the same side as your other fingers. At the start, the bar should be directly over your nose—if it isn't, slide yourself up or down on the bench until it is. Inhale, and unrack the bar from the supports. As you lower the bar to your chest, keep your elbows directly under the bar, rather than in front of or ahead of the bar. At the bottom of the movement, the bar should lightly touch your chest at nipple level. Return the bar to the starting position (it should actually travel up, as well as slightly back) by contracting your pectorals.

Always employ a competent spotter when performing any bench press variation.

A-2: LEG PRESS

Assume a seated position on the leg press machine with feet about shoulder width apart on the foot plate. Keep your lower back flat against the seat back at all times. Straighten your legs and release the safety mechanism (see the machine's instruction card for more details). Next, lower the foot plate toward you, allowing it to descend as low as you can without rounding your lower back. Pause; then push the foot plate back to the top position.

SECOND PR ZONE (15 MINUTES)

B-1: LAT PULLDOWN

Grasp the bar with your hands slightly wider than shoulder width apart, with palms facing away from your body. Next, pull the bar down toward your clavicle by contracting the latissimus dorsi (lats) and elbow flexor muscles. Return to the start position.

SECOND PR ZONE (15 MINUTES)

B-2: SUPINE LEG CURL

Lying faceup on the floor, position your heels on the ball and pull your toes up toward your shins as you pull your shoulder blades back and down. Contract your gluteals until your body is in a straight line from ankle to shoulder. Keeping your hips tall, pull your heels in toward your gluteals. Let the ball roll back slowly as you straighten your legs. Keep your hips elevated for all repetitions.

THIRD PR ZONE (15 MINUTES)

C-1: STEPUP (LEFT)

C-2: STEPUP (RIGHT)

Perform these on a 14- to 16-inch bench or block. As you step up, keep the stress on the quads by making sure that the nonworking foot never rests on the floor. Your working knee should stay directly over the middle of the working foot. Complete all reps for first leg, rest, and complete the reps for the opposite leg.

FIRST PR ZONE (15 MINUTES)

A-1: MILITARY PRESS

Place a loaded bar on a rack at about your upper-chest level. Grasping the bar with both hands, lift it off the rack and support it on your shoulders as shown. From this position, drive the barbell up off the shoulders, vigorously extending arms overhead until your elbows are locked. Keep your back and legs locked throughout. Reverse this motion to complete the rep.

FIRST PR ZONE (15 MINUTES)

A-2: STANDING DUMBBELL CURL

From a standing position, keep your elbows locked to your sides as you flex your elbows maintaining a palms-forward position throughout. Return to the starting position, keeping your elbows stabilized (motionless) throughout the exercise.

SECOND PR ZONE (15 MINUTES)

B-1: CLOSE-GRIP BENCH PRESS

Lie faceup on the bench, placing both feet on the floor. Grasp the bar such that your hands are 18 to 24 inches apart, and make sure your thumbs are wrapped around the bar, rather than on the same side as your other fingers. At the start, the bar should be directly over your nose—if it isn't, slide yourself up or down on the bench until it is. Inhale and unrack the bar from the supports. As you lower the bar to your chest, keep your elbows directly under the bar, rather than in front of or ahead of the bar. At the bottom of the movement, the bar should lightly touch your chest at nipple level. Return the bar to the starting position (it should actually travel up, as well as slightly back) by contracting your pectorals.

SECOND PR ZONE (15 MINUTES)

B-2: STANDING HAMMER CURL

This is simply a standard curl performed with a thumbs-up grip, which increases the involvement of the brachialis muscle of the forearm. From a standing position, keep your elbows locked to your sides as you flex your elbows, maintaining a thumbs-up grip throughout. Return to the starting position, keeping your elbows stabilized (motionless) throughout the exercise.

THIRD PR ZONE (15 MINUTES)

C-1: LUNGE (LEFT)

C-2: LUNGE (RIGHT)

Stand with your feet hip width apart and take a long step forward (the length of the step should be such that your front shin is perpendicular to the floor at the bottom of the lunge position. Next, lower your body until your rear knee almost touches the floor. Pause; then complete the rep by pushing yourself back to the starting position. Keep your chest up and eyes forward. Your rear heel will come up off of the floor as you sink down.

CHAPTER TEN

THE 3–5 METHOD CONTRAST CYCLE

AS GREAT AS EDT IS, IT'S IMPORTANT TO REALIZE THAT IT'S ALSO VERY intense. You'll need a break from it from time to time. As the old saying goes, "Any form of training that is intense enough to make you grow is also intense enough to cause overtraining." EDT is no exception. Therefore, occasional periods of less demanding workouts are warranted. My general recommendation is to train EDT-style for 8 weeks and then take 1 week completely off, followed by 3 weeks of the 3–5 method. These occasional 3-week cycles are still challenging, but in a different way from EDT—so you'll find that they'll feel almost like a vacation!

The 3–5 method has been around forever but has been popularized recently by my friend and colleague Pavel Tsatsouline. Understanding this method couldn't be simpler: You'll train 3 to 5 days per week, using 3 to 5 exercises per workout, doing 3 to 5 sets of 3 to 5 reps per exercise, with 3 to 5 minutes of rest between sets. On all exercises, choose a weight that is challenging but not overwhelming. Each time you repeat a workout, try to use slightly more weight for the same set-rep format.

Here's an example of an effective training split for the 3–5 method.

MONDAY

A: SQUAT

(3 SETS OF 5 REPS)

Position the barbell on the support pins inside of a power rack so that the bar is level with your midchest. Place safety pins on each side, at a position slightly lower than your intended deepest position. Place your hands evenly on the bar (a close grip with elbows under the bar will allow for a more upright posture). With your feet squarely under the bar, lift it from the rack by extending your legs.

Next, step back just enough to avoid bumping the rack during the exercise, and position your feet at approximately shoulder width. The weight should remain centered over the back half of your feet, not on the heels or toes. Slowly descend into a near-bottom position, keeping the torso and back erect so that the hips remain under the bar at all times. Do not allow the hips to drift backward or the torso to drift forward. Rise out of the squat position, following the same path that you descended. Your torso and back should remain erect, and your hips should remain under the bar throughout the ascent.

MONDAY

B: BENCH PRESS

(4 SETS OF 5 REPS)

Lie on the bench, placing both feet on the floor (if this causes your lower back to arch, find a lower bench or place your feet on solid blocks to elevate them, allowing your back to lie flat). Grasp the bar so that both hands are equidistant from the center, making sure to wrap your thumbs around the bar, rather than keeping them on the same side as your other fingers. When you start, the bar should be directly over your nose—if it isn't, slide yourself up or down on the bench until it is. Inhale, and lift the bar from its supports. As you lower the bar to your chest, keep your elbows directly under the bar, rather than in front of or ahead of the bar. At the bottom of the movement, the bar should lightly touch your chest at nipple level. Return the bar to the starting position (it should actually travel up, as well as slightly back) by contracting your pectorals.

And remember, *always* employ a competent spotter when performing any bench press variation.

MONDAY

C: PRONE LEG CURL

(5 SETS OF 5 REPS)

The best leg curl machines feature a raised or arched bench, which facilitates a greater range of motion throughout the movement than a flat bench. Keep your head down and pelvis stabilized (i.e., immobilized) during the movement. The knees should be aligned with the axis of the machine. If the roller behind the calves seems to slide up or down during the movement, adjust your alignment by sliding forward or back on the bench. Curl the weight by contracting the hamstrings. Pause at the top, and then lower yourself to the starting position.

WEDNESDAY

A: LAT PULLDOWN

(5 SETS OF 5 REPS)

Assume a seated position under the bar. Pull the bar down to your clavicle (never behind the neck, which lessens the exercise's benefit and increases the possibility of neck injuries). This exercise is completed by simultaneously flexing at the elbows, retracting the shoulder blades, and slightly arching the back. Think of pushing the chest to the bar rather than pulling the bar to the chest. Do not lean backward during the pull.

WEDNESDAY

B: STIFF-LEG DEADLIFT

(5 SETS OF 5 REPS)

Set up a barbell slightly higher than knee level (use a power rack, or set the barbell on blocks). With your palms facing your body, grab the bar with a shoulder-width grip, and step back just enough to clear the rack. Inhale, slightly bend at the knees, and begin the movement with your body weight over your heels. Allow the bar to descend while you make sure it maintains contact with the front of your body. While descending, keep your back arched, and allow the glutes to move rearward. Do not look up, but instead maintain a forward-looking focus. Always maintain a slow, controlled movement with this exercise. Never perform it rapidly or explosively.

C: DIPS

(5 SETS OF 5 REPS)

Descend slowly and under complete control. Maintain a vertical torso for more shoulder and triceps involvement, and a forward lean to increase pectoral recruitment. Be careful not to exceed your shoulder's range of motion. Return back to the top position by contracting your pecs, deltoids, and triceps. If needed, you can create extra resistance by adding weight plates to a belt or by placing a dumbbell between your calves.

WEDNESDAY

D: BARBELL CURL

(5 SETS OF 5 REPS)

Without moving your shoulders, lock each elbow firmly in place at your sides. Flex your elbows, raising the bar in an arc until both arms are completely flexed, with the bar pressed against your chest. Lower through the same arching path.

A: SQUAT

(3 SETS OF 5 REPS)

Position the barbell on the support pins inside of a power rack so that the bar is level with your midchest. Place safety pins on each side, at a position slightly lower than your intended deepest position. Place your hands evenly on the bar (a close grip with elbows under the bar will allow for a more upright posture). With your feet squarely under the bar, lift it from the rack by extending your legs.

Next, step back just enough to avoid bumping the rack during the exercise, and position your feet at approximately shoulder width. The weight should remain centered over the back half of your feet, not on the heels or toes. Slowly descend into a near-bottom position, keeping the torso and back erect so that the hips remain under the bar at all times. Do not allow the hips to drift backward or the torso to drift forward. Rise out of the squat position, following the same path that you descended. Your torso and back should remain erect, and your hips should remain under the bar throughout the ascent.

FRIDAY

B: BENCH PRESS

(4 SETS OF 5 REPS)

Lie faceup on the bench, placing both feet on the floor. Grasp the bar such that both hands are equidistant from the center, and make sure your thumbs are wrapped around the bar, rather than on the same side as your other fingers. At the start, the bar should be directly over your nose—if it isn't, slide yourself up or down on the bench until it is. Inhale, and unrack the bar from the supports. As you lower the bar to your chest, keep your elbows directly under the bar, rather than in front of or ahead of the bar. At the bottom of the movement, the bar should lightly touch your chest at nipple level. Return the bar to the starting position (it should actually travel up, as well as slightly back) by contracting your pectorals.

Always employ a competent spotter when performing any bench press variation.

C: PRONE LEG CURL

(5 SETS OF 5 REPS)

The best leg curl machines feature a raised or arched bench, which facilitates a greater range of motion throughout the movement, as opposed to a flat bench. Keep your head down and pelvis stabilized (or immobilized) during the movement. The knees should be aligned with the axis of the machine. If the roller behind the calves seems to slide up or down during the movement, adjust your alignment by sliding forward or back on the bench. Curl the weight by contracting the hamstrings. Pause at the top, and then lower yourself to the starting position.

EDT SCORE SHEET

EXERCISE	EXERCISE
5 Total:	5 Total:
4 Total:	4 Total:
3 Total:	3 Total:
2 Total:	2 Total:
1 Total:	1 Total:
TOTAL:	**TOTAL:**

- Use one sheet per PR Zone.
- In the "exercise" fields, enter the name of the antagonistic exercises you'll perform during the PR Zone.
- Once you begin the PR Zone, enter a slash every time you perform a set, using the appropriate field (if you do a set of 5, enter it in the "5" field, and so forth).
- In each field, calculate your subtotals.
- Toward the bottom, calculate your final totals for each exercise.

(A free printable 8½-by-11 version of this form can be found online at www.EDTSecrets.com/scoresheet.pdf.)

CORE-INTENSIVE TRAINING PROGRAM

PEOPLE VARY GREATLY IN TERMS OF WHERE THEY TEND TO STORE body fat. This is what leads to the various myths about lower abdominal training—since most people (males in particular) tend to store their fat on the lower abdominal wall, they end up with the idea that somehow they aren't training their "lower abs" correctly.

Nothing could be further from the truth. The *most* important concept to understand is that regardless of people's individual differences, the overwhelming majority of people can greatly improve the appearance and functioning of their abdominal muscles. I sincerely hope that this guide proves to be an important first step in that direction.

Myth One: If You Have a Wide, Blocky Waist, There's Nothing You Can Do about It

FACT: This myth leads some to avoid ab work altogether (see Myth Four) and others to stick to high reps in hopes of "toning" their waistlines (see Myth Two).

While it's true that there's not much that can be done about a genetically wide waist (typically due to a wide pelvis), you *can* create the illusion of a narrower waist by putting more mass on other muscle groups, particularly your legs and shoulders. When you create additional lower- and upper-body width, your waist will actually be narrowed by comparison. So, in many respects, squats and military presses may do more to improve the appearance of your waist than any number of crunches.

Myth Two: **High Reps Are for Tone; Low Reps Are for Bulk**

FACT: Just to set the record straight, "tone" refers to a partial, involuntary state of contraction—typically the result of a recent workout or other stress to the muscle. Problem is, if your abs are covered by fat, it won't matter how toned they are, because you won't be able to see them anyway! So once again, we're back to the simple truth that having great abs comes down to energy management. You need to coax your body into reducing its fat stores by reducing calories and by doing more physical work.

Now, back to reps. At the end of the day, it's not so much how many reps you do, or how many sets you do, but how much *work* you do. In other words, for any given muscle or muscle group, if you lift, say, 135 pounds for 3 sets of 20 repetitions in 15 minutes (which most people would call "high reps"), you'd get a total volume of 8,100 pounds (135 × 60 reps) for that 15-minute workout.

On the other hand, if you perform 6 sets of 10 with that weight, you'll also get 8,100 pounds. Or if you lift 185 pounds for 4 sets of 11, you'll get a total volume of 8,140 pounds. So, as you can see, there are many ways to skin a cat. On this issue, I agree with Nike: Just do it!

Myth Three: **You Have to Focus on Your Lower Abs, Which Are the Hardest Area to Develop**

FACT: Ah, the dreaded "lower abs" myth! If you're like most people, Mother Nature prefers to deposit your abdominal fat below your navel. This leads to the never-ending search for the perfect low-ab exercise. But wait! Unfortunately, there is no direct metabolic pathway to the lower portion of your rectus abdominis muscle and the fat layer on top of it.

Bear with me as we do a bit of anatomy here. Physiologically, the rectus abdominis muscle spans the distance from your sternum to your pelvis—this muscle does not have "lower" and "upper" sections (although it does have between two and four tendinous "intersections" along its length—hence the term "six-pack").

Interestingly, the lower and upper sections of this muscle do indeed have separate nerve supplies, leading some to speculate that one can devise specific training drills that target the lower abs. I disagree. Assume a crunch position on the floor, and place one hand on your upper abs and the other on your lower abs so that you can feel the muscles contract as you perform a crunch. As you curl yourself up into the crunch, you'll feel both portions of your rectus abdominis contract simultaneously.

And, as noted before, even if you could preferentially target your so-called lower abs through a particular exercise, who cares? The fat on top of your abs (or anywhere else, for that matter) will decrease only when you've created an energy deficit by decreasing calories and/or increasing your activity levels. Most ab exercises burn relatively few calories compared with big, compound exercises, such as squats, deadlifts, bench presses, and pullups.

Myth Four: Too Much Ab Work Gives You a Big Waist

FACT: Very few individuals are capable of significant muscular hypertrophy of the abdominal muscles, which could theoretically lead to a larger waist. Why? First, these muscles have a relatively small proportion of fast-twitch muscle fiber (the type most capable of enlargement). Secondly, the architecture and tissue leverage of these muscles make them less capable of significant growth, compared with longer, better-levered muscles like the quads, lats, and hamstrings.

I suspect this particular myth stems from the current crop of elite bodybuilders, who possess distended abdomens (despite exceedingly low body fat levels)—this is most likely a function of anabolic drug use and is not a concern for those who do not use these drugs.

One interesting side note on waist size: Through heavy rows, squats, deadlifts, and back extensions, it is possible to significantly enlarge the lumbar extensors of the spine. This would increase your waist size; however, it would not lead to the appearance of a larger waist.

Myth Five: Crunches Are Better Than Situps for Isolating the Abs

FACT: It is true that situps involve more muscle groups than crunches. That's because a crunch involves trunk flexion only (the act of "rolling up" such that your spine leaves the floor one vertebra at a time), whereas a situp involves flexing at the hips (involving the hip flexor muscles, of course) once you've completed the act of trunk flexion. So, in essence, crunches primarily challenge the rectus abdominis muscle, and situps target the rectus as well as the hip flexor musculature.

Which is better? Neither, in my opinion. By all means, do them both, but remember that far more calories are burned by training larger muscle groups, such as the quads, hamstrings, lats, and pecs.

Myth Six: You Can (or Can't) Work Your Abs Every Day

FACT: The optimal frequency of any type of training is a function of two factors: how intensely you train and the total amount of training your body must recover from. Therefore, if your ab training sessions are super-grueling, it's probably best to train them two or three times per week. On the other hand, if your ab training is more on a "maintenance-level" schedule, it may be possible to train them every day without negative consequences.

One word of caution, however: Intense squats, deadlifts, and/or overhead lifts should be performed on fresh abdominal muscles. This is because during these lifts, the abdominals play a key role in raising intra-abdominal pressure, which functions to decrease pressure on the intervertebral disks in the lower back. If you perform, for example, heavy squats when your abs are tired from the previous day, you may significantly increase your risk of lower-back injury. This fact is partially responsible for the common practice of training abs at the end of a leg workout—this positioning ensures that your abs will be as fresh as possible during the subsequent leg workout.

As a related observation, it's sometimes interesting to examine the motivation behind one's training practices. In this case, what would motivate someone to want to perform abdominal work every day? In most cases, it's the misguided belief that large volumes of abdominal work will somehow reduce the size of the waistline (we've already covered this misconception in Myths Three and Five).

Myth Seven: You Should "Suck In" Your Navel during Squats and Deadlifts to Help Stabilize Your Spine

FACT: The idea behind this rather impractical advice stems from the fact that drawing the navel toward the spine helps to activate the deepest layer of your abdominals (called your transverse abdominis), which functions to protect the spine (by increasing intra-abdominal pressure, mentioned earlier) during heavy lifting.

Sounds like a no-brainer right?

Well, here's my take on it: The transverse abdominis (also called the TVA) does in fact increase intra-abdominal pressure, which is a very good thing. Your body has its own innate intelligence, and it already knows how to protect your spine during heavy lifting, without the rather counterintuitive maneuver of drawing your navel inward when squatting. As it turns out, virtually everyone will instinctively hold their breath and "bear down" (called a Valsalva maneuver) when attempting a heavy lift. So it basically comes down to this: Does it make more sense to use a natural, instinctive maneuver, or something that feels completely unnatural? I'll leave that decision to the reader; however, I do know that when push comes to shove and you really need to stabilize your lower back during a heavy lift, your body will use the Valsalva maneuver every time.

By the way, a decidedly low-tech way to discover the best way to do things is to look at people who do it most successfully—success isn't an accident, after all. In the case of squats and deadlifts, I am not aware of a single elite-level powerlifter or Olympic-style weightlifter who sucks in his or her navel when performing heavy squats or deadlifts.

THE BOTTOM LINE ABOUT YOUR WAISTLINE

Genetic constraints notwithstanding, whether or not your abs are enviable or regrettable is mostly a function of your overall body fat percentage, which is most effectively lowered

FORM RECOMMENDATIONS FOR ABDOMINAL EXERCISES

- **In order to train the main abdominal muscle (called the rectus abdominis), you'll need to flex your trunk, which means you'll take the curvature out of your lower back—an exception to the neutral-spine rule discussed earlier.**

- **As you perform crunches, try this awareness exercise: Place one finger on your lower sternum, and one finger from your other hand on your pubic bone. Now crunch. You'll notice your fingers drawing toward each other. At a certain point, however, you'll notice that you can continue your upward movement by "hingeing" up from your hips, even though your fingers never get any closer to each other. This means that other muscles (most notably your hip flexors) have been recruited into the job. That's okay. However, if you want to focus the brunt of the work on your abs, stop curling up when your pelvis and sternum have reached their closest position.**

- **During any form of crunch or situp, become aware of and avoid the tendency to curl your chin toward your upper chest. Think: "Keep space between the chin and chest."**

- **During any form of crunch or situp, visualize curling up one vertebra at a time. As you develop your awareness, see if you have a tendency to curl up in "chunks." This may indicate flexibility issues in your spine. Keep working on it!**

- **Rotational exercises, while effective for developing the oblique muscles, can sometimes exacerbate lower-back problems. Make sure you have a good reason to do them (a tennis or golf player, for example, might benefit from such exercises).**

through an intelligently designed exercise and nutritional program, which in turn must be supported by a healthy lifestyle and smart time- and energy-management strategies. Issues such as lower versus upper abs, high versus low reps, and situps versus crunches (among other issues) really account for less than 2 percent of the final result. My recommendation is to continue with your ab work, but keep things in perspective: If you want great abs, you've got to lower your body fat level through sound nutrition and smart, intense training for all of your major muscle groups.

In my opinion, it is neither wise nor preferable to have a training program that is devoted exclusively to abs—at least in the sense of using traditional "isolation" exercises for these muscles. First, there's no way the abs could tolerate so much volume for very long, and second, your other muscle groups would become detrained from lack of attention. Therefore, this is a whole-body program with extra emphasis on core musculature.

FIRST PR ZONE (15 MINUTES)

A-1: SQUAT

Position the barbell on the support pins inside of a power rack so that the bar is level with your midchest. Place safety pins on each side, at a position slightly lower than your intended deepest position. Place your hands evenly on the bar (a close grip with elbows under the bar will allow for a more upright posture). With your feet squarely under the bar, lift it from the rack by extending your legs.

Next, step back just enough to avoid bumping the rack during the exercise, and position your feet at approximately shoulder width. The weight should remain centered over the back half of your feet, not on the heels or toes. Slowly descend into a near-bottom position, keeping the torso and back erect so that the hips remain under the bar at all times. Do not allow the hips to drift backward or the torso to drift forward. Rise out of the squat position, following the same path that you descended. Your torso and back should remain erect, and your hips should remain under the bar throughout the ascent.

FIRST PR ZONE (15 MINUTES)

A-2: CHINS (ON CHIN/DIP ASSIST UNIT)

Grasp a chinning bar with an underhand grip approximately shoulder width apart. From a hanging position, pull yourself up until your chin clears the bar. Reverse this motion to return to the starting position. Avoid flexing from the hips when performing pullups or chins.

This exercise is performed the same way as pullups, except that chins are performed with your palms facing toward you, which increases biceps involvement. The closer the grip, the more the biceps are involved. Chalk or lifting straps may be used to secure a good grip.

SECOND PR ZONE (15 MINUTES)

B-1: DUMBBELL TURKISH GET-UP (LEFT)

B-2: DUMBBELL TURKISH GET-UP (RIGHT)

Lie faceup on the floor holding one dumbbell straight above you. Turn to the opposite side and use your free arm to help you into a squat position. From there, stand up and then reverse the movement. When you finish all reps for the left arm, switch to the right arm.

SESSION 2

FIRST PR ZONE (15 MINUTES)

A-1: DUMBBELL SNATCH (LEFT)

A-2: DUMBBELL SNATCH (RIGHT)

Begin by squatting low over a dumbbell. Maintain a locked and rigid lower back. Your feet should be about shoulder width apart. Grasp the dumbbell and tighten the abdominal muscles. In an explosive and continuous motion, accelerate the dumbbell upward until your arm is straight and locked. The dumbbell should travel close to the body and not swing out or away. Briefly hold it above the head, and then bring it down to the starting position. If necessary, you may assist the descent by using the opposite hand.

SECOND PR ZONE (15 MINUTES)

B-1: REVERSE TRUNK TWIST ON BALL

With a secure handhold on two upright poles, lie such that the arch of your back rests directly on the stability ball. Raise your legs so that they are in a position perpendicular to the floor.

Keeping your hips flexed and shoulders stabilized, allow your legs to fall to your left until (ideally) they are at the same distance to the floor as your hips. Then return to center and continue down to the opposite side–this is 1 repetition.

SECOND PR ZONE (15 MINUTES)

B-2: HIGH CABLE CRUNCH

Stand with a rope attached to a high-cable pulley, feet hip width apart, knees slightly bent. Facing away from the machine, grasp the rope with both hands at forehead height, elbows bent, upper arms parallel to floor and each other. Maintaining arm position, flex forward in a crunch motion without changing hip angle. Complete the rep by reversing this action.

Note: **If you're performing this at a lat pulldown station, you can stabilize yourself by pinching the seat with your legs.**

RESOURCES FOR SUCCESSFUL WEIGHT TRAINING AND NUTRITION

ATLANTIS FITNESS EQUIPMENT: After using virtually every type of weight-training equipment in existence and finding many that are good, I think only Atlantis can be considered "great." The design, workmanship, and professional service are of the highest standards. Atlantis equipment is also very competitively priced. Call toll-free at 877-454-2285, or go to www.atlantis-fit.com.

BIOTEST: Leading manufacturers of high-quality nutritional products for hard-training bodybuilders and athletes. Call toll-free at 800-525-1940 or go to www.biotest.net.

CHARLESSTALEY.COM: The author's personal Web site. Learn more about EDT, as well as distance coaching, personalized training, and the author's many books and videos.

DRAGON DOOR PUBLICATIONS: Provides the world's most effective methods for high performance, radiant health, and peace of mind. Find them on the Internet at www.dragondoor.com.

THE INTERNATIONAL SPORTS SCIENCES ASSOCIATION: The ISSA acts as a teaching institution and certification agency for fitness trainers, athletic trainers, martial arts instructors, and medical professionals in every field of health care. ISSA hosts seminars in most states as well as numerous countries around the world. The ISSA has set new standards in exercise assessment, nutritional planning, fitness instruction, sports medicine practice, and post-rehabilitation training. ISSA's certification and continuing education programs are universally recognized. For more information, call 800-892-ISSA (4772), or go to www.issaonline.com.

IRONCOMPANY.COM: IronCompany is a leading supplier of home and commercial exercise and fitness equipment for residential use and schools and GSA (General Services Administration) military contracts. Since 1998, they have been committed to providing excellent-quality home and commercial fitness equipment and outstanding customer service. Call toll-free at 888-758-7527, or go online at www.ironcompany.com.

IRONMIND ENTERPRISES: Great source of hard-to-get equipment, such as "bumper" plates for the Olympic lifts, oversize bars and dumbbells, grip-strengthening devices, and much more. Call 530-265-6725, or go online at www.ironmind.com.

SMARTFUEL: Whether you're pushing bike pedals, computer keys, or a baby stroller, eating right is essential for the everyday athlete. SmartFuel's innovative nutrition products conveniently supply specific amounts of energy and nutrients to help the everyday athlete power through the high-pace of a busy day. Call toll-free at 888-768-FUEL (3835), or go online at www.SmartFuel.com.

WEIGHT TRAINING THAT REALLY WORKS: Coach Staley demonstrates the principles and nuances of Escalating Density Training in DVD format. Call 800-519-2492, or go online at www.EDTSecrets.com.

INDEX

Boldface page references indicate photographs. Underscored references indicate boxed text.

D

P

Q

R

S

T

ALSO AVAILABLE FROM RODALE BOOKS…

Men'sHealth®

THE ABS DIET

By David Zinczenko with Ted Spiker

Want to strip away belly fat and have beach-ready abs all year round? Let *Men's Health* editor-in-chief David Zinczenko teach you how.

"*The Abs Diet* is a sensible eating and exercise plan, not a fad diet. The Abs Diet Power foods and the Abs Diet Workout are designed to make you fit, healthy, and lean for life. If you want to get on top of your game, this is where you start. Remember: "Don't cheat yourself, treat yourself."

—The Rock, movie star

THE ACTION HERO BODY

By Jørgen de Mey

Trainer to the stars Jørgen de Mey reveals the unique program he has used to transform the bodies of Action Hero film stars Angelina Jolie, Ben Affleck, and many others!

"I was told to work out with Jørgen by movie producer Jerry Bruckheimer. I didn't feel I needed personal training at the time, but I was wrong. What I learned from Jørgen will keep me in shape for the rest of my life. Any time I'm on the beach and a girl mentions how in shape I am, I know I have Jørgen to thank."

—Jerry O'Connell, actor

MEN'S HEALTH® HARD BODY PLAN

By Larry Keller and the editors of *Men's Health*

Get bigger shoulders, bulging biceps, ripped abs, a leaner torso, and strong legs in just 12 weeks—guaranteed! The *Men's Health Hard Body Plan* gives you three cutting-edge 12-week full-body muscle plans, revolutionary quick-set paths to power, and a sensible eating plan to keep you fueled. Say goodbye to love handles and say hello to a body that will make heads turn!

MEN'S HEALTH® THE BODY YOU WANT IN THE TIME YOU HAVE

By Myatt Murphy

Burn fat, build muscle, and stay fit—no matter how much (or little) time you have! With 120 fat-burning, muscle-building workouts organized by how many days a week you have to exercise, and subdivided into 10-, 20-, 30-, 45-, and 60-minute exercise blocks, you'll be able to develop a weekly fitness routine that works with your schedule—not against it!

THE NEW HIGH INTENSITY TRAINING

By Ellington Darden

Built on the HIT philosophy of harder, briefer exercise, Darden's book is packed with the explosive-growth workouts and advanced bodybuilding programs you need to get fast results at home or in the gym. Now is the time to blend the old HIT with the new HIT to trigger…Explosive Muscular Growth! Start growing today.

Available wherever books are sold.

RODALE
LIVE YOUR WHOLE LIFE™

Now I Kn

What's Under t

by MELVIN AND GILDA BERGER

SCHOLASTIC INC.

New York Toronto London Auckland Sydney
Mexico City New Delhi Hong Kong Buenos Aires

Cover: © David B. Fleetham / SeaPics.com; page 1: © David B. Fleetham / SeaPics.com; page 3: © Jeff Greenberg / Peter Arnold, Inc.; page 4: © Astrofoto / Peter Arnold, Inc.; page 5: © Lynn Funkhouser / Peter Arnold, Inc.; page 6: © Gregory Ochocki / Photo Researchers, Inc.; page 7: © Schafer & Hill / Peter Arnold, Inc.; page 8: © Marty Snyderman / SeaPics.com, small: © Ron & Valerie Taylor / SeaPics.com; page 9: © Remi Benali/Corbis; page 10 left: © IFA / Peter Arnold, Inc., top: © Mark Strickland / SeaPics.com, bottom: © Doug Perrine / SeaPics.com; page 11 top: © Masa Ushioda / SeaPics.com, bottom: © Doug Perrine / SeaPics.com; page 12 left: © Doug Perrine / SeaPics.com, right: © Amos Nachoum / SeaPics.com; page 13: © Gary J. Adkison / SeaPics.com; page 14: © Kelvin Aitken / Peter Arnold, Inc.; page 15: © Tom Brakefield / Corbis; page 16: © Mike Johnson / SeaPics.com; page 17: © Hiroya Minakuchi / SeaPics.com; page 18: © Shedd Aquar /Lines Jr / SeaPics.com; page 19 left: © Doug Perrine / SeaPics.com, right: © Mark Strickland / SeaPics.com; page 20: © Doug Perrine / SeaPics.com; page 21: © Doug Perrine / SeaPics.com; page 22: © Jeff Rotman / SeaPics.com; page 23 inset: © Andrew J. Martinez / Photo Researchers, Inc., large: © Doug Perrine / SeaPics.com; page 24: © J.Kassanchuk / UNEP / Peter Arnold, Inc.; page 25: © Doug Perrine / SeaPics.com; page 26 large: © E. R. Degginger / Photo Researchers, Inc., inset: © Robert P. Carr / Bruce Coleman Inc.; page 27: © Thinkstock Images (RF) / PictureQuest; page 28: © Garo / Photo Researchers, Inc.; page 29: © Phillip Colla / SeaPics.com; page 30: © Peter Pinnock; Gallo Images / Corbis; page 31: © Jeffrey L. Rotman / Corbis; page 32: © Michael Patrick O'Neill / SeaPics.com

ISBN 0-439-88853-0

18 17 16 15 14 13 12 14 15 16/0

Printed in the U.S.A.
First Printing, September 2006
Book design by Nancy Sabato

It is very deep.

What lives under the ocean?

Fish do.

Some are large.

And some are small.

Some come in beautiful,
bright colors.

Look who's swimming by — a shark!

One kind of shark has a head like a hammer.

DID YOU KNOW?

Sea turtles can swim faster than humans!

Here is a giant sea turtle.

Sea turtles have flippers, not legs.

Can you see the biggest
animal in the ocean?

DID YOU KNOW?

A blue whale is as long as three school buses!

It is the blue whale.

Here come some of the
smallest animals in the ocean.

This is a tiny sea horse.

A baby dolphin swims
with its mother.

They jump up.
They dive down.

Let’s go deeper into the ocean.

DID YOU KNOW?

Sponges are animals!

Sponges live down here.

Corals live here, too.
What else lives here?

DID YOU KNOW?

Millions of coral make up a coral reef.

Lots of fish and other animals live on the coral reef.

Do you see the crab?

Don’t get in its way!
It may pinch you if you do.

Seaweeds are plants.
Some are very small.

Some are very, very long.

MILLIONS of animals and plants live in the ocean.

The ocean is their home!

GLOSSARY

Coral: A tiny sea animal. Corals leave their stony skeletons behind when they die.

Coral reef: An underwater structure built up from the skeletons of huge numbers of tiny animals called coral.

Crab: A sea animal with a hard shell, eight legs, and two claws.

Dolphin: A kind of small whale with a long snout.

Fish: An animal that swims and breathes under the water.

Ocean: Huge bodies of salt water. Oceans cover most of Earth.

Sea horse: A small fish with a head like a horse and a curling tail.

Sea turtle: A large turtle that lives in the sea or ocean.

Seaweed: A plant that grows under the ocean. Seaweed can be any size from tiny to giant.

Shark: A fish with very sharp teeth. Sharks eat other sea animals.

Sponge: A sea animal. A sponge's body has many holes to take in water and food.

Whale: A large sea animal that looks like a fish — but is not a fish. Whales are mammals that breathe air.